THE STORY OF THE SCENE

THE INSIDE SCOOP ON FAMOUS
MOMENTS IN FILM

ROGER CLARKE

Methuen Drama

3 5 7 9 10 8 6 4 2

First published in Great Britain in 2009 by Methuen Drama

Methuen Drama
A & C Black Publishers Ltd
36 Soho Square
London W1D 3QY

A CIP catalogue record for this book is available from the British Library

ISBN 978 1 408 10987 8

Typeset by Margaret Brain, Wisbech, Cambs
Printed and bound in Great Britain by Latimer Trend & Co Ltd

THE STORY OF THE SCENE
THE INSIDE SCOOP ON FAMOUS MOMENTS IN FILM

ROGER CLARKE

CONTENTS

PREFACE

'Story of the Scene' is an occasional column written for *The Independent*. I've been writing it since 2004, when I was the resident film critic on 'The Information' section. I've been contributing to *The Independent* on and off for over 15 years; in that time the Internet and the extended market for DVD boxsets (with their voice-overs and making of documentaries) has made it far easier to find out about your favourite films and how they are made. All the same there's still plenty of room for fresh interviews and new insights, and in this regard I've been in contact with Nic Roeg, Park Chan-wook and John Boorman, to name but a few.

One of the things that became obvious very early on is how people on the same production can tell you entirely contradictory accounts of the same event, so I've done my best to steer a sensible path when this happens. Many of these insights are new – you'll not read anywhere else about what really happened when Nic Cage ate a cockroach in *Vampire's Kiss*, or how dummies used in *The Mission* caused a police scare; how Stanley Kubrick became obsessed with the male rape scene in *Deliverance*, or how the live octopus-eating scene in *Oldboy* was filmed.

What happens behind the scenes is often far more bizarre and revealing than anything that appears in the finished film.

Roger Clarke
April 2009

FOREWORD

It may be human nature – albeit a rather unflattering aspect of it – that encourages us to feel good when we know a little bit more than our friends. Few things compare to being able to listen to a remarkable, mind-boggling snippet of trivia and then deftly produce another, better, more outrageous one and shouting, 'Trump!' It's something I do on a regular basis, despite the fact that my wife is adamant it is one of my very worst habits; and despite the more pertinent fact that occasionally I have embellished or added little snippets to my own snippet to make it a little juicier, a little more memorable, a lot more impressive. Also, perhaps, human nature. But that's not to say I haven't been on the receiving end of some fabulous, spurious titbits myself.

Here are just a few of the many outrageously weird stories about the making of some of my favourite films I have been told over the years. Someone once 'reliably' informed me that a munchkin tied a noose around his or her little neck and jumped off a turret in *The Wizard of Oz* when filming was over. If you freeze the frame at the right moment and look very closely (and I'm sure watching it in BluRay would help no end), you can supposedly see a very small person dangling from a rooftop as Dorothy & Co. skip happily away from Oz. Not true, of course, but a great story.

Someone else informed me that Arnold Schwarzenegger slept with the female actor playing the alien hooker with three breasts in *Total Recall*, insisting she kept the prosthetic chest on during the act. *Definitely* not true, although who could have blamed him?

People have insisted that the mechanical shark in *Jaws* killed a technician when a power surge made it chomp unexpectedly during a rehearsal; and that everyone involved in the making of *The Exorcist* has either died themselves, or lost someone close in a bizarre, inexplicable accident. Perhaps best of all, a reasonably trustworthy associate remains adamant that a certain leading lady in Hollywood was born a hermaphrodite, and has only ever dated or married men who seek out that special something in prospective partners. I cannot confirm or refute that one, but suspect that it's unlikely – just as the rumour going around that Cher asked her surgeon to remove two of her ribs to make her even more slender, and then turned the ribs into salad-tossers, is absolutely not true. I asked her.

But if you don't have first-hand access to the great and the good, then getting to the truth is even harder. This is thanks in no small part to that sprawling, delightful nest of rumour and gossip that is the Internet. Like a ball of wool that's been abandoned and played with by a whole army of curious kittens, it's all but impossible to untangle. Facts that started as jokes or just as theories have been reported and reheated so many times that they have the feel and weight of truth, even when they lack that one vital attribute of actually having happened.

Which is why this volume – created by esteemed film journalist and stickler-for-the-truth, Roger Clarke – is both a vital weapon in the battle against this rising tide of disinformation, and a cracking good read. Finally, the truth about the filming of the chest-bursting scene in Alien! At last, someone has got to the bottom of whether or not Nic Cage really did eat a live cockroach for that key scene in *Vampire's Kiss!* And I can now reliably inform those who might be interested exactly how many live octopi actor Choi Min-sik had to chow down on while making that Korean masterpiece, *OldBoy*. All of those facts are contained inside, in a delightfully portable, eminently readable, thoroughly enjoyable collection. Thanks, Roger.

(By the way, did I ever tell you that a friend of mine knew someone who worked on *Robocop*? Apparently they actually turned Peter Weller into a cyborg ...)

Jonathan Ross
July 2009

ACKNOWLEDGEMENTS

With thanks to:

David Lister, Roger Alton, Tim Robey, John Boorman, Adam Roberts, Iain Smith, Mark Kermode, Wonjo Jeong, June Lee, Robert Bierman, Park Chan-wook, Sarah Bemand, John Dunning, Nick Fox, Fay Weldon, Karen Krizanovich and Stephen Fry. Special thanks to Jenny Ridout for commissioning this book, Inderjeet Garcha, Suzi Williamson and everyone at A & C Black. Finally, to Jonathan Ross for his generosity and good-humour; ask a busy man if you want something done. Extra special thanks to Kim Newman.

Dedicated to Simon Su

ALIEN
1979
DIRECTED BY RIDLEY SCOTT

Raised from a baleful, technology-induced sleep, the crew of the mining spaceship *Nostromo* stop to investigate a mysterious distress signal. In the carcass of an ancient craft on a stormy planet they discover a strange cargo of mephitic giant eggs. John Hurt's character Kane bends over to peer in; one egg is opening itself at the top like the doors on a missile silo. In a mucilaginous flash, an organism has attached itself to his face.

Taken back to the ship Kane remains unconscious until the creature, shaped like a strangulating hand, appears to wither and fall off. But in the mess hall of the *Nostromo* he convulses – and a gruesome second-stage alien bursts from his chest cavity in an arterial spray of bloody tissue.

It's been said that Ridley Scott concealed this innovative slaughter-house moment from 28-year-old *ingénue* Sigourney Weaver and her co-stars, hoping to catch their actual expressions of fear and revulsion as the special effect breached its cavity. 'As I walked on set,' recalled Weaver years later, 'I should have noticed everyone [on the crew] was wearing raincoats.'

But contrary to myth the chestbuster scene was not a surprise to all the actors; everyone knew something was about to happen, they just didn't have the specifics. All the same, Scott – manning the camera as he did for 80 per cent of the film – was especially delighted by Veronica Cartwright's genuine expression of horror.

Designer Roger Dicken had originally wanted a gorier moment, with the pseudo-foetal alien ('a degenerate plucked turkey', as he characterised it) clawing its way out with its own little hands. Scriptwriters don't usually get involved, hands on, in special effects, but Dan O'Bannon actually helped design and make the original facehugger. It was the birth scene of what O'Bannon was later to call 'a movie about alien interspecies rape'.

The special effects, some of the most innovative in film-history, won an Oscar. At the source of the innovative design was Swiss artist HR Giger who, like O'Bannon, was involved in one of the great what-ifs of film history – Alejandro Jodorowsky's *Dune*, never made. Interestingly Giger's models for both the facehugger and the chestburster

were a great deal less successful than his design for the fully grown adult alien, and all had to be modified.

Hurt was never supposed to be in the movie. He was brought in well after shooting actually began, hired at short notice to replace veteran Hammer Studios actor Jon Finch. Curiously, Finch had to bow out after experiencing severe chest pains. 'There I was on the set of *Alien*,' he recalled much later. 'I had been shooting for two days. I had my face cast and my chest measured for when the alien [chestburster] comes out. Suddenly ... I was in intensive care.'

The chestbursting scene has proved to be gold dust for parodists – sometimes involving John Hurt himself, who, with characteristic good humour, reprised it for Mel Brooks in *Spaceballs* in 1987. Not so surprising when you discover that the original design for the Giger chestburster, when presented to the production team, induced fits of laughter. Gloomy, gothic, introverted, chronically haunted by bad dreams, Giger was distinctly unamused.

AMADEUS
1984
DIRECTED BY MILOS FORMAN

In one of the great scenes from Milos Forman's *Amadeus*, Tom Hulce as Mozart is as good as conducting himself into the grave as his rival and nemesis Salieri (an Oscar-winning performance from F Murray Abraham) plots his end from a theatre box above. It's the premiere of his opera *Don Giovanni*, staged in Prague in 1787, and we're nearing the end of the film and the untimely demise of Mozart himself.

In a voice-over narration, embittered court composer Salieri tells how the ghostly father-figure of the opera is about to drag his disreputable son down to hell. Is it Mozart's own father? Salieri will use this specific filial horror to destroy him.

Forman returned to his native (then) Czechoslovakia in 1983 to direct this sequence in the actual theatre where Mozart himself conducted the premiere of *Don Giovanni*, its overture written mere hours in advance. With the country still, at the time, under the sway of a Stalinist elite, Forman's moves were closely monitored. Captured for posterity are the 30 or so secret policemen who masqueraded as extras in the audience, the auditorium lit only with natural light and some 6,000 candles.

Forman, quite naturally, was at pains to ensure that the historic Tyl Theatre didn't get burned down on his watch, and during all the rehearsals none of the candles and torches were lit. Some 40 firemen had been hired to stand at 15-foot intervals all around the building, constantly monitoring for sparks, flames and incipient conflagrations. Everything went smoothly and Forman finally gave the orders for all the candles to be lit. The cameras rolled.

In the opera, Don Giovanni is onstage when the animated statue of the lately deceased Don Pedro the Commendatore crashes through a wall and confronts him. As the scene progresses, Don Giovanni's constant scurrying around kept brushing feathers past a candelabra burning on the table.

In real life, the attending firemen looked on as the feathers smouldered for a while before finally catching fire. But still they didn't move.

Finally one of the firemen slid over to the director and whispered in his ear, 'Mr Forman, do you know that one of your actors is on fire'? Forman quickly bellowed 'Cut!'

The conventional explanation for this unwillingness to act by any of the firemen is that they were in the thrall of a police-state mindset; don't do anything unless ordered. But there is another possible reason. One of Forman's early films, the one which led to his quitting Czechoslovakia, was *The Fireman's Ball* (1967). It was condemned by the Communist Party, which sent along party stooges to stand up after a screening and condemn the director's view of the 'heroic firemen'.

But all the real local firemen also stood up at the same event and said that, in fact, what they had witnessed on screen was quite accurate; their colleagues were indeed frequently too drunk to put out fires. Forman was a hero to the firemen of Czechoslovakia. They were in awe of him, and not about to step in to ruin one of his films.

APOCALYPSE NOW
1979
DIRECTED BY FRANCIS FORD COPPOLA

Sam Mendes's film *Jarhead* involves a scene where the US marines in Iraq are watching the *Ride of the Valkyries* section from *Apocalypse Now*. It's the helicopter attack scene on a Vietnamese coastal village, Wagner blaring from specially mounted loudspeakers. The troops in the more contemporary conflict whoop with pleasure at this scene of high-octane military devastation. Coppola's film, however, is much more ambiguous about the wartime activity it depicts, even if it was written by the gung-ho John Milius.

Apocalypse Now is based on a novella by Joseph Conrad. Set in the Belgian Congo, it shows the search of a shady military operative (Martin Sheen, in later life a prominent pacifist) sent to terminate 'with extreme prejudice' a former army colonel who has gone AWOL deep in the jungle – Col Kurtz (Brando, fat).

Coppola's filming in the Philippines became infamous, almost more picked over than the film itself. There was the out-of-control budget, the drugs and heart attacks and monsoons and dealings with the Marcos regime, mostly recounted in a superb documentary, *Hearts of Darkness*, made by Fax Bahr and George Hickenlooper with Eleanor Coppola in 1991. The *Ride of the Valkyries* scene occurs relatively early in the movie when Cpt Willard and his PBX crew (they are heading up-river) hitch a lift with a helicopter cavalry unit commanded by Robert Duvall as Lt Col Kilgore.

The music is from *Die Walküre* (Act III, Scene 1) and Kilgore uses it to instil mortal dread in the Vietnamese as his attack-helicopters swoop in low from the sea. Some of this scene has been extended in the recent *Apocalypse Now Redux* edit. The AirCav lands after a torrent of missile launches and Kilgore sends off one of Willard's crew to surf while the situation is mopped up by a napalm attack from circling jets. 'I love the smell of napalm in the morning,' are his immortal words.

The Loach helicopters were borrowed by Coppola from the Philippine airforce. Every night they were repainted and sent off to attack communist rebels in active service. 'We never knew the next morning how many would come back and in what condition,' recalled Walter Murch, the film's celebrated editor. The helicopters were then repainted as US issue.

It turns out that Coppola only had eight helicopters to play with; ingenious use of camera angles alone makes it look like the requisite 23. The recording of the helicopter sounds was later made with the US coastguard in Washington using three different helicopter models, and the sound of the napalm comes from a recording made by the Swiss Army of its use. The use of sound in *Apocalypse Now* remains an often overlooked benchmark in the industry: the system Murch and Coppola developed became the basis of Dolby Stereo.

BASIC INSTINCT
1992
DIRECTED BY PAUL VERHOEVEN

In the late 1980s Joe Eszterhas was the most famous scriptwriter in Hollywood. He was rock-and-roll. His films *Jagged Edge* and *Flashdance* had made a fortune and his ballsy, vulgar confidence was deemed thrilling by the cosseted studio bosses. There was no one like him in Hollywood – he was one of the few scribes perfectly happy to eyeball the biggest players until they coughed up vast sums of money. His status peaked in the early 1990s when he was paid $3 million for *Basic Instinct*.

The film is best remembered for the scene in which Sharon Stone crosses and uncrosses her legs. She is wearing no knickers. This has always been held up as evidence of Eszterhas's essential crassness.

In the film Sharon Stone, who was a late casting for the role after many other actresses turned it down, plays a multi-millionaire authoress who has written a book that describes an ice-pick murder. By a strange coincidence her musician boyfriend dies by the same method, and suspicion naturally falls on this glossy bisexual *femme fatale*. Michael Douglas plays the investigating San Francisco detective who becomes steadily besotted with her, and it is during a police interrogation, in which she stylishly smokes a cigarette and wears a tiny white dress, that the scene occurs.

When the film came out, it was picketed by gay rights campaigners – but unlike director Paul Verhoeven, Eszterhas met them to discuss their concerns. It soon became clear that he and Verhoeven had not seen eye-to-eye during the shoot. Verhoeven had admitted that, despite two further drafts by other hands, Eszterhas's script would be shot as delivered. Verhoeven never quite got over that admission.

Joe Eszterhas has long since fallen into obscurity, with his unmade scripts still turning up in the fire-sales of bankrupt production companies. He made so much money that, turning his back on the industry, he retired, finding time to write an entertaining auto-biography called *Hollywood Animal* which reveals an unexpected detail about the infamous leg-crossing scene, voted sexiest 'leg moment' on screen in a 2004 poll. One evening, it seems, he was startled to be asked by his 15-year-old son how he had come up with the idea. Eszterhas had to swallow his pride and admit the truth: 'It wasn't in the script. It was Paul's idea.'

THE BATTLESHIP POTEMKIN
1925
DIRECTED BY SERGEI EISENSTEIN

It's one of the most analysed, most quoted single scenes in cinema –
the 'Odessa steps' sequence of *The Battleship Potemkin*.

In 1905 Russia, Czarist troops marched on unarmed civilians in the
Black Sea port. As Ronald Bergan observed in *Eisenstein: A Life in
Conflict*, audiences have since believed that 'the scenes on the Odessa
steps ... [are] a faithful reconstruction of an actual event'. In fact, the
event never took place.

The movie was ordered up by the Russian film agency, Sovkino, to
honour the 20th anniversary of the naval insurrection which anticipated the Marxist-Leninist revolution in Russia by a decade. The film
starkly observes the poor conditions which the average sailor was
expected to endure (the ship has limped home following the war with
Japan). The crew mutiny and gain the support of the local people in
the port, who send them out supplies.

In the famous six-minute sequence, Cossack troops confront the
townsfolk with a long march down a flight of steps, firing on the fleeing
citizens who scatter before them. A legless man rushes to escape. An
elderly female teacher is shot in the face (an image that was to
influence Francis Bacon). Another woman is shot dead trying to

protect a baby in a pram – which then bounces down the steps, out of control.

The pram sequence has been copied and parodied by Brian De Palma in *The Untouchables* (1987) and by the Zucker brothers in the third of their *Naked Gun* films. Woody Allen's *Bananas* also pays it homage. The reality of the actual uprising was very different from the film version: the townsfolk did not in fact victual the rebelling warship. The Potemkin was not greeted by other navy ships as portrayed in the movie, and the mutiny did not spread to the fleet.

Eisenstein was actually sued by a Potemkin mutineer who claimed the director had stolen his story. The case actually went to court in Odessa, where Eisenstein was able to prove that the details he created were entirely a fiction of his own making.

For a short while the film was shown with a written introduction by Leon Trotsky. On its release it played to half-full theatres, and the Soviet authorities exaggerated its box-office figures; it wasn't until it was sent to Berlin that it became a wild success. Joseph Goebbels considered *Potemkin* 'without equal in the cinema ... anyone who had no firm political conviction could become a Bolshevik after seeing the film'.

The movie was banned in the UK until 1954, and was X-rated until 1987. The original score was composed by Edmund Meisel, but in recent years it has proved a popular choice for live re-scoring. The Pet Shop Boys composed a new soundtrack in 2004. It was played live in Trafalgar Square, a celebration, perhaps, of the brand new steps built there by Mayor 'Red' Ken Livingstone the year before.

THE BIRDS
1963
DIRECTED BY ALFRED HITCHCOCK

The climactic sequence of *The Birds* by Alfred Hitchcock takes place in the attic of a Bodega Bay house, where Tippi Hedren takes the full brunt of thousands of wild birds as they begin a terrifying attack. The scene has proved immensely influential in the horror genre and led directly to the premise of *Night of the Living Dead*, filmed some years later.

Tippi Hedren was Hitchcock's discovery – one in a long line of celestial blondes he liked to use and abuse on-screen. She plays the shallow socialite Melanie Daniels who encounters a young lawyer, Mitch Brenner, in a San Francisco pet shop. Stung by his sarcastic remarks she tracks him down to Bodega Bay where she gives him some caged lovebirds from the shop and stays the night with local schoolteacher Annie Hayworth. Soon after, massed seagulls and other birds start to attack human beings. At the Brenner family farm, windows are boarded up as the birds gather outside. But Hedren, upstairs in an attic bedroom, undergoes a savage assault as they find a way in.

Originally it wasn't supposed to be Tippi Hedren in the attic – the schoolteacher played by Suzanne Pleshette was the intended victim of the beaked attack in those first drafts. There were no trick shots used in the scene (despite the film being absolutely packed with them – 371 in all), yet it took a week to film. Hedren had to endure live seagulls being thrown at her and tied to her arms and legs with elastic bands and threads: a drawn-out and dangerous ordeal.

Original scriptwriter Evan Hunter had not designed it to play as a major scene, but the script was amended by Hitchcock himself. Much of the effectiveness lies not just in the obvious distress of Tippi Hedren, but in Hitchcock's clever use of the slicing sound of the birds' wings.

When Tippi Hedren finally retired it was to run an animal sanctuary in California, dedicated to the natural enemies of birds – cats.

BLADE RUNNER
1982
DIRECTED BY RIDLEY SCOTT

The climactic scene of *Blade Runner* involves the convergence of three novels, a famous building and a key piece of improvisation.

Ridley Scott's film was based on Philip K Dick's fiction *Do Androids Dream of Electric Sheep?* Around the same time, William Burroughs's script entitled *Bladerunner* (adapted from a novel by Alan E Nourse about a surgeon who sells surgical instruments illegally) was doing the rounds. Scott bought the script just so he could use the title.

The film depicts a hellish future of corporate police states and ruined climates. Genetically engineered human beings known as 'replicants' are rising up against their human masters and some have travelled secretly to earth. Harrison Ford is a cop trained to track them down and kill them.

Towards the end of the movie Harrison Ford leaves his car and walks towards a well-known LA landmark called the Bradbury Apartments. The interior of the building is filmed at its real location in South Broadway; its extensive ironwork, imported from France on the whim of an eccentric millionaire in 1893, sets the mood of noirish intrigue and menace.

When Ford's character gets to the top of the Bradbury he immediately finds himself in a fight to the death with a replicant played by Daryl Hannah (that's a male gymnast stand-in doing the back-flips). Then Rutger Hauer arrives. He pursues Ford, and as Ford seems about to plunge off the building to his death, delivers some famous lines including 'all those moments will be lost in time, like tears in rain'.

Hauer had been supposed to deliver a much longer scripted speech. However at 3 a.m., with dawn not far off, he asked Scott to visit him in his trailer to listen to lines he had written during a meal a little earlier. Scott immediately agreed to their inclusion, describing them as 'beautiful'.

It's the building, though, that really sets the scene – and it has a bizarre story attached to it. It was the brainchild of real-estate mogul Louis L Bradbury, who hired a junior draughtsman, George Wyman, to build it for him. Superstitious and a bit crazy, Wyman is said to have consulted his dead brother via Ouija Board before going on to develop the building according to the principles lain down by another futuristic

novel – *Looking Backward* by Edward Bellamy, published in 1887. At the opposite end of the spectrum to *Blade Runner*, it envisaged a Marxist utopia by the year 2000.

Scott had only stumbled on the Bradbury by chance, according to production designer Lawrence G Paull, while they were looking for a 'decrepit building'. 'We trashed it with high-tech,' he said later, using post-production techniques to age it and adding a canopy with big columns on the outside. In fact the Bradbury Building was already quite well-known in the business: you can see it in Joseph Losey's *M*, and it houses PI James Garner's office in *Marlowe*. Its use in *The Outer Limits* TV episode *Demon with the Glass Hand* is usually flagged up as a key source for *Terminator*.

BLUE VELVET
1986
DIRECTED BY DAVID LYNCH

The scene where Frank rapes torch-singer Dorothy, watched by Jeffrey standing hidden in a clothes closet through the slatted grill of the closet door, is one of the most disturbing in the hypnopompic cinema of David Lynch. It was the first scene in the film that Lynch shot with actor Dennis Hopper as the devilish and malevolent Frank.

Lynch had initially resisted the casting of Hopper, who had a reputation at the time for being difficult, and it wasn't until he received a call from casting director Johanna Ray confirming that Hopper was safely on the wagon that he contemplated the idea. In a well-known piece of Hollywood lore, Hopper rang up Lynch after reading the script and shouted 'I am Frank!' down the phone. It's a story he enjoys telling.

'I was caught in a bind,' recalled Lynch in conversation with author Chris Rodley for his book, *Lynch on Lynch*. 'I didn't want to know anybody like Frank – and yet for the film I had to have that person. Dennis was Frank, but luckily he was someone else too.' Lynch originally met Isabella Rossellini in a New York restaurant; soon after he cast her in *Blue Velvet* and they later dated for an extended period.

There are many unnerving aspects to this particular scene, mostly in the saintly visage of Isabella Rossellini as the masochistic Dorothy, so creepily evoking her mother Ingrid Bergman in her many Joan of Arc films (a figure for whom the actress had a lifetime obsession). Rossellini's obvious delight in being roughed-up by a demented hoodlum resulted in the picketing of London cinemas by women's groups when the movie came to the UK.

Much of the speech used by Frank was in fact scripted by Lynch, though Hopper decided to add more. He also influenced Lynch's decision to abandon his original idea of Frank getting high on helium; the plastic mask he clamps to his face is purely oxygen. 'Until the last minute it was going to be helium,' recalls Lynch, 'to make the difference between "Daddy" and the baby that much more. But I didn't want it to be funny.'

Talking to *Vanity Fair* in 1987, Rossellini offered a curious insight into the rape scene. 'When we were filming it, David couldn't stop laughing – he had to grab hold of himself not to disturb the scene.' For the director at least, it contained the pure helium of comedy.

BONFIRE OF THE VANITIES
1990
DIRECTED BY BRIAN DE PALMA

2nd Unit director Eric Schwab had worked for Brian De Palma for many years by the time they came to shoot *Bonfire of the Vanities*. Very early on in the production process he was shooting the scripted landing of an Air France Concorde flight into New York's JFK Airport. De Palma bet the younger man $100 that he couldn't make the shot interesting enough to merit inclusion in the movie. Goaded by the challenge, Schwab went away and began one of the most elaborate preparations for a simple single short shot in Hollywood history.

It was June 12th 1990, the 38th day of production. In the novel, author Tom Wolfe hadn't specified which plane brought the character Maria (played by Melanie Griffiths) back from Europe, and immediately Schwab set about arranging a scene in which Concorde would land at JFK at precisely the moment that the Empire State building and the setting sun were all in one single frame.

This particular date was chosen because it was the only date when the locus of the sun would enable all the elements to come together. Schwab had gone so far as to contact the programmers of a specialist Casio computer to double-check his calculations on the earth's orbit relative to the sun, with the exact longitude and latitude factored in.

Throughout the spring Schwab spent weeks walking round the airport with his location scout Bruce Frye, deciding on the elusive perfect place to make the shot. After clearance from the Port Authority and the Federal Aviation authority (who insisted that Warners take on insurance liability for millions), Schwab and his photographer Andrew Laszlo calculated that they had a 30-second window for the plane to descend, at precisely the right angle, as the sun dropped behind the city skyline.

Five cameras arranged with different lenses were situated by runway 13L, and 20 minutes beforehand the specially flown-in Air France Concorde took off and began circling the airport before making its descent on cue.

Schwab spent anxious moments scanning the skies with a pair of binoculars; the slightest mishap and months of planning would be lost. But the plane landed perfectly. The result was astonishing in visual terms; the plane seemed to hover over the Empire State building and

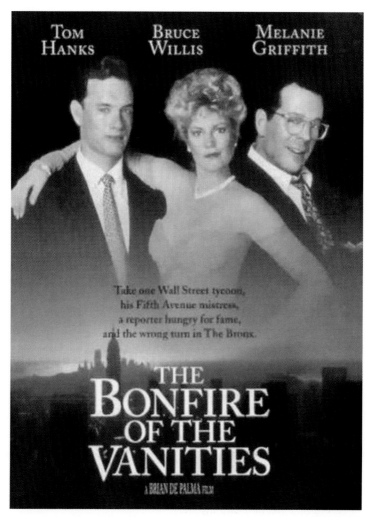

New York city, and looked 'like an Aztec bird' in the description of Julie Salamon in *The Devil's Candy*, the definitive account of the movie's troubled production and its subsequent box-office failure.

BREATHLESS
1960
DIRECTED BY JEAN-LUC GODARD

Modern movies begin with Jean-Luc Godard's *Breathless*, with Jean Seberg as the American *ingénue* in Paris who dashes off with insouciant cop killer Jean-Paul Belmondo in his stolen car. The production credits are a roll-call of the filmmakers of *La Nouvelle Vague* (French New Wave).

Godard's co-conspirators had set up *Cahiers du Cinema* (a formerly influential French film magazine). They used their time as professional critics to dream. They wanted to make their own films. Director François Truffaut had come up with the basic story idea; Claude Chabrol was the supervising producer; and director Jean-Pierre Melville appears as a celebrity novelist being interviewed. He has a testing gender-wars perspective. 'Two things are important in life – for men, women, for women, money.'

In one scene, Godard himself plays an informer. Forty years on, though much imitated, it still breaks all the rules. The jump-cuts, the spatial alienation, addresses to camera, a roving 35mm camera anticipating Steadicam – these were just some of the techniques that Godard used in his first feature (the only one of his films, he says, which made any money).

Way before the Danish movement of Dogme '95 (which supposedly abhors the use of effects), only natural lighting was used. Legends abound about the shoot, including the use of a wheelchair as a camera dolly.

Godard later admitted that the only scene he actually wrote in advance was the famous opening in the Champs Elysées – 'for the rest I had a pile of notes'. But it is the 20-minute-long love scene in the Hôtel de Suède that was perhaps the most revolutionary thing in the film. Both actors are smoking; Belmondo is on the bed and Seberg beside it.

The light from the window envelops them in a cloud. She quotes Faulkner: 'Between grief and nothing, I will take grief.' Belmondo says he will take nothing since 'grief is a compromise'. She poses in front of a Renoir poster, a painting of a girl, demanding to know who is the prettier. Finally they make love.

In this scene and throughout the film, Godard uses his famous jump-cuts – a jarring technique that was later explored in the films of

Quentin Tarantino and Wong Kar-Wai. Moments of dialogue or action are suddenly and peremptorily ended and stuck to another moment of action or dialogue.

This was all part of Godard's aim to go against the conventions of what he called 'dad cinema' – but they do say that necessity breeds invention. Though there are antecedents to this technique in the films of Eisenstein and even Méliès, Godard actually stumbled on the idea when the film came in 30 minutes too long. He simply snipped out everything that was 'boring', with little regard to the obvious rules of continuity.

Many years later, Jean Seberg met a tragic end, committing suicide in a car in the suburbs of Paris. Her body was not found for many days.

BULLITT
1968
DIRECTED BY PETER YATES

Steve McQueen is in his Dark Highland Green 1968 GT Ford Mustang. The mafia hit men are in their Black 1968 Dodge Charger 440 R/T. What follows, through the streets of San Francisco, is the greatest car-chase sequence ever filmed.

Steve McQueen plays Detective Frank Bullitt in this adaptation of Robert L Pike's novel *Mute Witness*. The car chase wasn't in the original script, which had been made with Spencer Tracy in mind before McQueen and producer Philip D'Antoni got hold of it. They changed the main character from a Boston-based, ice-cream-eating policeman to McQueen's lean and mean detective. They moved the location. Then they hired British director Peter Yates on the basis of his work filming a realistic car chase in *Robbery* (1967).

McQueen based his character partly on the homicide detective Dave Toschi, who became well-known in San Francisco for his detection work on the Zodiac serial killings. That custom-made shoulder-holster is based on Toschi's. McQueen, a speed-freak who raced semi-professionally, hired stuntman Bud Ekins (who also did the motorcycle jump in *The Great Escape*) for the most difficult bits. Otherwise the majority of the driving was completed by McQueen in a souped-up car with racing shocks and GR70 tyres. The lack of dialogue, the cool, understated soundtrack and the number of profiles and close-ups were quite revolutionary at the time.

Practice for the chase scene took place at the race track at Cotate, California, and the ten-minute sequence took two weeks to film. It might have been even more spectacular, visually, had the local city not refused the use of Golden Gate Bridge. But it's the very use of backstreets that makes the sequence so special and real.

Ford provided Warners with two cars of each make, and three of them were trashed. The less-damaged car, with 40,000 miles on the clock, was sold to a Warners employee from the editing department. McQueen tried to buy it for himself when it was sold again in 1977, but failed.

McQueen's Mustang still resides, by all accounts, in a hay barn in Ohio River Valley. Without the original Nardi steering wheel, its sides punched through from where the camera-mounts were bolted on, an

expert who saw it recently estimates that it would cost $10,000 to restore.

The chase, the inspiration for several generations of video games, frequently reached speeds of over 110 mph. You can tell who is driving the Mustang by the position of the mirror – when it's visible, that's McQueen behind the wheel. When down, Ekin.

In this clever website, you can follow the scene with real-time GPS tracking: www.seero.com/video/Steve_McQueen_3

BUTCH CASSIDY AND THE SUNDANCE KID
1969
DIRECTED BY GEORGE ROY HILL

The bicycle scene represents a key moment in *Butch Cassidy and the Sundance Kid*, even if, these days, its soft-focus, long-shadowed autumn idyll and sugar-candy over-dubbed music by Burt Bacharach feels dated. In a brief snatch of dialogue, Paul Newman (as the outlaw Butch Cassidy) and love interest Etta (Katharine Ross) draw up to the shack where they're hiding out. With a flourish, 'Butch' announces 'meet the future', gesturing towards the bicycle he is riding. There follows an extended sequence where Etta rides on the handlebars and Butch plays the fool – before being chased off by an enraged bull.

Shot in Utah, Colorado, Mexico and New Mexico, *Butch Cassidy and the Sundance Kid* begins with a form of disclaimer saying 'most of what follows is true'. Butch was the train-robber whose first big heist was the 1867 train robbery at Grand Junction in Colorado. It's generally accepted that Butch was gunned down after a run-in with the Bolivian police force in San Vicente in 1908, but to her dying day his sister claimed she visited him in Utah some 16 years later. Incredibly this same sister used to visit the film set and by all accounts was charmed by Newman's version of her brother; 20th Century Fox later managed to persuade her to endorse the movie when it was released.

The song *Raindrops Keep Fallin' On My Head* was written by Burt Bacharach and Hal David with Bob Dylan in mind, and is a rare example of a Bacharach song that retained its dummy title (the nonsense written to service a tune). It was eventually crooned by one BJ Thomas, recorded while he was suffering from a bout of laryngitis.

The scene was a moment of genuine happiness for the two actors, most particularly Katherine Ross who had fallen out with director George Roy Hill for the most peculiar reason. On the first day of shooting, the DP Conrad Hall was setting up a train robbery scene only to find that he had five cameras and only four operators. He asked actress Katherine Ross to operate one of the cameras, and she did. Director Hill said nothing, but was fuming. Later he banned her from set unless she was in a scene. She's happy here because the whole scene was filmed by the 2nd Unit, with no trace of Hill on-set.

Newman performs all his own stunts except where he crashes backwards into the bull's pen; the person you see there is the

cinematographer. And the bull? His name was Bill. He was flown to Utah from Los Angeles for this one scene, and a pepper-spray was applied to his testicles to make him mad enough to charge the Butch Cassidy character.

CAPE FEAR

1962
DIRECTED BY J LEE THOMPSON

When Robert Mitchum first got news that he was to film *Cape Fear* in Savannah, he exclaimed: 'They railroaded me in that town, man! They may have a warrant out for my arrest!'

Director J Lee Thompson could not have known, when scouting for locations for his adaptation of John D Macdonald's pulp fiction *The Executioners*, that he would bump into Mitchum's less than salubrious past. The book is set in the Carolinas, but Thompson found that the town in Georgia fitted the bill perfectly. However, it transpired that when Mitchum was a footloose 15-year-old, drifting round America like some Woody Guthrie hobo smoking pot, taking rides on freight trains, he had indeed been arrested for vagrancy in Savannah and had served time on a local chain gang.

Mitchum was nearly not hired – Telly Savalas had done a very good screen-test – but in the end director Thompson and actor-producer Gregory Peck had plumped for wildman Mitchum after discussing the role with him. From the minute Mitchum moved into the local Desoto hotel he raised merry hell, immediately inviting into his suite a delegation of southern belle hairdressers who were having a convention in the same hotel. Thompson recalled however that Mitchum nursed a seething resentment for the town and had 'contempt for everyone there'.

Mitchum's character is a sadistic ex-jailbird called Max Cady, whose clever manipulation of the law allows him to terrorise and stalk the local attorney and his family who put him in jail. Gregory Peck plays the attorney in question. This was very much Peck's production and nobody had quite anticipated that Mitchum would steal the film, but steal it he did. Mitchum's channelled rage never seemed more brutal and more psychotic. 'You know I live this character,' he told the director. 'And this character drinks and rapes.'

The production had left Savannah for the climactic final scene, shot in Universal's back-lot lake. But in Mitchum's mind he was still there, in his nemesis town. Cady is now in the final showdown with the attorney and his family as they drift along a night-time river on an unsecured boat. Mitchum was completely demented by this point. He had already roughhoused actress Barrie Chase in earlier scenes, so much so that

the day's shooting had to be stopped, but these scenes were no-holds-barred: he nearly drowned Gregory Peck. 'We had to send a man in to get Peck up,' recalled the director. *Cape Fear*'s most uncontrolled sequence, and the last scene to be shot, involves Cady brutalising the attorney's wife, played by Polly Bergen. Most of the footage was too violent to use and Mitchum drew blood from the actress.

When the director called cut, Mitchum 'continued beating her up' and had to be pulled off.

CARRIE
1976
DIRECTED BY BRIAN DE PALMA

At last things seem to be working out for Carrie White. The bullied schoolgirl is going to the senior prom with the best-looking boy in the school. She's about to be crowned prom queen. But it's all a fix – her fellow teens are out to humiliate her. Few who have seen the sequence will forget that teetering bucket of blood set just above her head. Carrie's telekinetic revenge on just about everyone, and the six-minute slow-motion scene that proceeds it remains one of director Brian De Palma's most memorable scenes.

De Palma read Stephen King's first novel *Carrie* after a recommendation from a writer friend. After reading it he went out and bought the rights. He had another actress in mind for the lead, but knew Sissy Spacek already; she was married to film designer Jack Fisk who had worked with De Palma before. Eventually she was cast and Piper Laurie came out of retirement to play her demented mother.

The film was cheap to make at $1.8 million and with a 50-day shooting schedule. The special effects were organised by Gregory M Auer and the blood was made of something called karo syrup and food colouring, even though Sissy Spacek had volunteered to have actual pig's blood spilled on her. When Carrie returns home after her prom meltdown, and deals with her mother, the script had called for the house (designed by Spacek's husband) to be destroyed by a volley of rocks. In the end, however, Auer's machine for hurling the rocks – a kind of conveyor belt – proved not powerful enough to collapse the house, which had been built at half scale. The shoot was running late at 4 a.m. and the police had been called about the noise, so De Palma opted for simply burning the house down.

The dizzying camera effect at the prom was achieved by placing Sissy Spacek and William Katt on a platform that actually revolved in one direction while the camera dollied in another. The haunting music is by Pino Donaggio, who wrote the score for *Don't Look Now* and replaced Hitchcock composer Bernard Hermann after his sudden death. Donaggio had been recommended to De Palma by Jay Cocks, the music critic on *Time* magazine.

One of the oddest things about *Carrie* is how it shadowed a little-known production at the time called *Star Wars*. De Palma held joint

auditions with George Lucas, and many cast members read for both films, including Carrie's prom date William Katt for Luke Skywalker. However, in an interview with *Premiere* magazine Carrie Fisher denied she had ever turned down the role of Carrie. It had been claimed she wasn't prepared to do nude scenes; the rumour wasn't true. 'I love being nude,' she purred.

CASABLANCA
1942
DIRECTED BY MICHAEL CURTIZ

It débuted more than a decade earlier. Written in 1931 by New Jersey composer Herman Hupfeld, for the stage revue *Everybody's Welcome*, the song *As Time Goes By* became one of the most famous songs in film history – even if, despite the famous command from Humphrey Bogart's character Rick, Sam didn't actually 'play it' – and if the jealous composer of *Casablanca*'s musical score had had his way, the song would have been jettisoned altogether.

The making of *Casablanca* is one of the burnished legends of Hollywood, a piece of hackwork which just so happened to become a masterpiece. Humphrey Bogart is the owner of Rick's Café Américain in Casablanca under Vichy rule during WWII, and Ingrid Bergman plays his ex-lover who comes back into his life – briefly. When she turns up in his bar the pianist is asked, not without an edge of bitterness, to play their favourite song.

Rick's Café Américain was said to be modelled on Hotel El Minzah in Tangiers, and the bar itself is one of the only sets built from scratch in the entire film. Wartime privations had meant the cannibalisation of other movie sets; you may recognise the Paris train station from *Now, Voyager*.

The movie was based on an unproduced play called *Everybody Comes to Rick's*, co-authored by a high-school teacher called Murray Burnett while on summer vacation; it's said to have been inspired by a visit to the south of France and the witnessing of a black pianist in a café entertaining a group of Nazis and French refugees. Whether the musician was actually playing *As Time Goes By* is not recorded; it was however a favourite song of Burnett's.

Bogart never says 'Play it again, Sam'; he says 'You played it for her, you can play it for me. Play it!'. And as the pianist, played by Arthur 'Dooley' Wilson, launches into the famous rendition (without the first verse of earlier recordings) he is in fact miming. Wilson was an experienced nightclub singer but he was no pianist, and the playing you hear is that of one Elliott Carpenter performing just off-screen. Wilson would sneak occasional looks over Carpenter's keyboard to adjust his own pretence.

Max Steiner, who wrote all the other music in the movie, later tried to scotch the scene after filming was over, claiming it should be reshot with one of his own songs. Producer Hal B Wallis managed to deflect him by pointing out that Ingrid Bergman had now cut her hair short for *For Whom the Bell Tolls*, and it would not be possible to reshoot the scene.

You can see the real pianist of this scene featured in a little-known film from 1940. *Broken Strings* features Elliott Carpenter in the flesh discussing his music, and the suffering of his fellow African-Americans.

THE CHARGE OF THE LIGHT BRIGADE
1936
DIRECTED BY MICHAEL CURTIZ

The disclaimer 'no animals were harmed during the making of this film' can be traced back to the carnage of a single movie made during the 1930s. The death of nearly 50 horses using the infamous 'Running W' wire method caused such an outcry that the practice was banned forever. In his autobiography Errol Flynn was to claim that he himself had made a complaint to the Society for the Prevention of Cruelty to Animals, and 2nd Unit director B Reeves Easton, responsible for the excessive use of a technique that broke horses' legs, was sufficiently shamed to take his name off the credits.

The $1.2 million Warner Bros spectacular was filmed in California with the Sierra Mountains doubling as the Khyber Pass. Reuniting Olivia de Havilland and Errol Flynn after the success of *Captain Blood* (1935), *The Charge of the Light Brigade* was a simplistic love triangle which played fast and loose with historical fact, despite the studio's claim that technical adviser Sam Harris commanded a cavalry regiment in the second Zulu War and the Boer War. All the same the production design was so exacting that actual postage stamps from

the period were used in the film, despite never being seen on camera.

The 'Running W' was a simple, hideously cruel way to make horses stumble; wooden stakes were hammered into the ground just below the camera line and a wire attached to all four of a horse's legs. By varying the length of unspooling wire, the director could be sure at what point the horse would trip and fall, and the stunt-man too would know when to catapult himself forward over the horse's head. The horses, galloping full pelt in the key scene of the film, had no idea what was coming and the resulting fall broke legs and necks. But not only the horses were affected by the barely controlled chaos of the charge; one stuntman was killed when he landed on a broken sword.

During its filming the Hungarian director Michael Curtiz, struggling with the English tongue, shouted 'bring on the empty horses' to his crew when he wanted a host of riderless horses released into shot. Errol Flynn's co-star David Niven was sufficiently moved by this odd phrase, horribly resonant under the circumstances, to use it as the title of his autobiography written many years later.

The film was a great box-office hit and the next movie Flynn and De Havilland were to make together was *Gone with the Wind* (1939). In its own half-forgotten way, *The Charge of the Light Brigade* remains one of Flynn's most influential films in industry terms. That ill-advised spectacular in the San Fernando valley meant that Hollywood could never again act with impunity when it came to the safety of animals.

CHARIOTS OF FIRE
1981
DIRECTED BY HUGH HUDSON

When location manager Iain Smith turned up on the beach at St Andrews at 5 a.m., checking the conditions after a camera disaster the previous day, he assumed that the shoot would go smoothly this time around. The opening shot for *Chariots of Fire* showed the athletes in training, running through the sea, with St Andrews standing in for Broadstairs, Kent.

Since the film is set in 1924, all signs of modernity had been meticulously removed. Then Smith glanced up at the horizon and saw a modern British Navy frigate anchored offshore, dominating the bay. With only hours to spare, disaster loomed. He had to get rid of it.

Smith, who received an OBE in 2009 for services to the film industry and most recently produced the Angelina Jolie film *Wanted*, was then at the beginning of a distinguished career. 'These were the days before mobile phones,' he recalls, 'and I ran to the nearest red telephone box wondering – who do I phone?' He remembered that the RAF base in Leuchars had helped the production by providing camouflage netting; some local residents had refused to move their cars and the netting was used to disguised the vehicles' presence.

Smith called the duty officer at the base. He did his best to disguise the panic in his voice as the plummy tones of the duty officer sounded him out. What was his concern? A big navy boat? They were RAF. Not really their area, old chap. Once a boat was anchored, that was that. Was he sure he could see a naval vessel? Was he absolutely sure?

As Smith looked out across the bay through the glass panels of the phone booth, he noticed that the frigate was raising its anchor. 'Are you quite sure there's a boat out there?' persisted the duty officer. 'Yes, yes,' said Smith, 'I can see it right now.' Then to his astonishment, as he watched, still on the phone to the RAF, the frigate began to sail away. 'Are you quite sure?' continued the duty officer, calmly. Soon the boat had steamed off towards the horizon. 'No, there's no boat there,' admitted Smith. 'That's what I thought,' said the duty officer, who thanked him for his call, and put the phone down.

Smith never did discover the identity of his RAF benefactor. Besides, officially, no assistance had been given. The boat was never there. Though prefaced by a funeral sequence set in 1978 (interestingly

dropped from in-flight screenings), the film goes straight into this famous sequence, with Ian Charleson and Ben Cross, the music of Vangelis throbbing behind them, running through the tidal draw on the flat sands, accompanied by caddies from St Andrews golf course standing in as Olympians.

CHINATOWN
1974
DIRECTED BY ROMAN POLANSKI

Los Angeles private investigator Jake JJ Gittes, played by Jack Nicholson, has been hired to spy on the chief engineer of the city water department. There's a mystery as to why millions of gallons of water are being sluiced away from reservoirs under cover of night – in the middle of a drought.

So here is Gittes nosing round what is supposedly the Lake Hollywood water reservoir built by real-life Water Commissioner Walter Mulholland in 1925. He's seen by the security guard called Claude Mulvihill. Walking beside him is a sinister character with a rolling stride played by director Roman Polanski in cameo. Jenson grabs Nicholson. Polanski whips out a flick-knife and sticks it up Nicholson's nose. 'You're a very nosy fella, kitty-cat,' says Polanski.

When repeatedly asked about this scene in later years, Polanski and Nicholson, bored with giving the same answer, often pretended that what is shown on screen, over the next few seconds, really happened. Polanski slits Nicholson's nostril with his knife and the blood goes everywhere over his face. But how was it done?

The filming of *Chinatown* had been a predictably fractious business, with Polanski flying into rages with Nicholson and rowing with Faye Dunaway. Though they were to remain friends, something of the Nicholson/Polanski tension on-set freights the scene, which was filmed at Point Fermin at Paseo del Mar in southern LA. When Nicholson says, as the diminutive bow-tied director ambles towards him, 'Hello Claude, where d'you get the midget,' there's a slightly personal sting to the remark.

In turn Polanksi played mind games with Nicholson; Nicholson knew that Polanski had designed the prop-knife himself and that if the hinge faced the direction he was going to wrench it, the knife would fold safely back into the handle. If it wasn't correctly placed, it would genuinely cut Nicholson's nose. On each take, Polanski would flip the knife over and over till it wasn't clear whether it was safe. That's genuine fear and apprehension in Nicholson's eyes.

In fact it's quite clear how the trick was done if you look closely at Polanski's hand holding the prop knife, which would have had a small reservoir of fake blood in the handle and a tube out of sight to deliver

it. Just before he jerks the knife away, you see his thumb move slightly to the left to activate the button which was to eject the blood.

Chinatown was the last movie that Polanski was to make in the US. In 1977 he was arrested on a child molestation charge over events which had apparently taken place in Jack Nicholson's LA home. After pleading guilty and spending 42 days in prison for psychiatric assessment, Polanski skipped bail and fled to France, where he has remained ever since. A 2008 documentary on the case raised so many questions about the behaviour of the presiding judge that Polanski has launched an application for a judicial review.

A CLOCKWORK ORANGE
1971
DIRECTED BY STANLEY KUBRICK

It's not unknown for an actor to complain about their treatment during the making of a movie. But spare a thought for Malcolm McDowell. During the making of *A Clockwork Orange* during the bitter winter of 1970–71, he suffered broken ribs and nearly drowned in beef consommé (that dirty water in a trough is in fact soup). One scene stands out, however. McDowell is suffering. Genuinely suffering.

Stanley Kubrick adapted his film from the novel by Anthony Burgess, and even though the main character is 15 in the book, Kubrick was determined to make the film with 27-year-old Malcolm McDowell (who had caused a sensation with his rebellious teenager in *If...* a few years earlier). Having secured the film rights from the Rolling Stones (Jagger himself had intended to feature as the lead) he duly cast McDowell.

McDowell's character Alex DeLarge is a youth addicted to violence and rapine, and when he is eventually caught and imprisoned he is offered aversion therapy treatment after a period of good behaviour. This fictional aversion process is called the Ludovico Technique and is based on the principles of Russian scientist Ivan Pavlov.

Essentially DeLarge is strapped into a straightjacket and then into a chair where he is kept completely motionless; a piece of standard surgical equipment called a lidlock is fixed to his eyes so he is unable to close them. A scientist is obliged to irrigate his eyes with constant eyedrops whilst DeLarge is forced to watch a succession of violent and fascistic film scenes. After injection with an experimental drug, the plan is to create a visceral feeling of nausea whenever he is tempted to commit an act of violence.

Generations of students at Brunel University in Uxbridge have joked about the on-campus filming of *A Clockwork Orange* (including comedienne Jo Brand, who even says she went there because of it) and especially the infamous Ludovico Technique. The scene, which has been parodied in *The Simpsons*, referenced in the TV series *Lost* and endlessly looted for music videos by the likes of Duran Duran and Guns 'n Roses, has a terrifying vividness to it even today.

McDowell received local anaesthetic for the duration, and in spite of (or possibly because of) this, he scratched the cornea of his left eye.

It was a serious injury but Kubrick refused to stop filming – 'I'll favour your other eye,' he reassured his agonised actor. 'He's a genius but … I wonder about his humanity,' McDowell later said of his love-hate relationship with the man.

Kubrick later withdrew the film from distribution, frightened that it was being used to glorify violent behaviour, though it was never technically the subject of any ban.

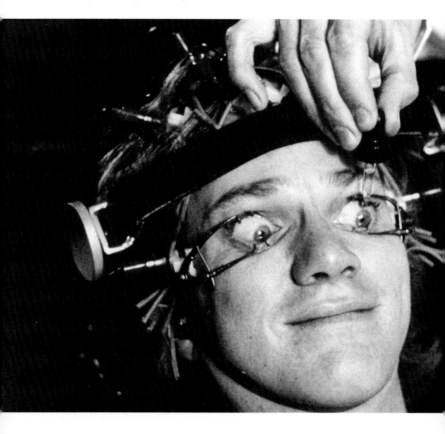

THE CONQUEROR
1956
DIRECTED BY DICK POWELL

What is it about the landscape in the opening scene of the John Wayne film *The Conqueror* that drove Howard Hughes to buy up every print of the film, bribe Richard Nixon and spend the last paranoid days of his life in a darkened room watching it over and over again?

It was a film originally intended for Marlon Brando, but early in 1954 John Wayne was in a business meeting with RKO producer Dick Powell when he happened to pick up a script-summary sitting on Powell's desk. Powell was intrigued by his interest and saw no reason to turn down one of the biggest box-office draws of the day. But despite Wayne's insistence that he would study with a voice coach, he turned up at the location in Utah's Escalante Desert completely unprepared, proceeding to speak all his lines in his usual Iowa drawl. The film has gone down as one of the most hilarious miscastings in Hollywood.

The story is of the early years of Genghis Khan. Wayne and his fellow Caucasian actors, their eyebrows shaved and the tops of their heads treated with spirit gum to provide slanted eyes, are charging down the hillside to intercept a caravan winding its way through the valley below. They are waving the wrong kind of swords and wearing the wrong kind of clothes, but never mind – there's haughty Susan Hayward as the Tartar Princess Bortai lying seductively on a divan, and Genghis intends to have her for himself.

In real life it was the other way round. Hayward and Wayne had houses rented for the shoot either side of the street in St George, Utah, and on many evenings Hayward would get drunk and roll over to the Duke's house, on one occasion kicking off her high heels and shouting 'let's fight over him' to Wayne's future wife Pilar Pallete.

But what was it about this movie shoot that so haunted its producer, Howard Hughes? Try the radioactive dust which had blown down from the Yucca Flats atomic site in Nevada. Over the 13 weeks of shooting, the actors and crew were covered in it – and to make matters worse, 60 tons of strontium-90-laced dirt was shipped to a Hollywood studio for some later scenes.

Of the 220 persons involved with the film, 91 succumbed to cancer – including Wayne, Hayward, Powell and Agnes Moorehead. A Utah radiologist Dr Robert Pendleton later classified it as 'an epidemic'.

Hughes was supposed to have felt 'guilty as hell' about the poisoning of his cast and crew; according to the book *Citizen Hughes* by Michael Drosnin he even bribed Richard Nixon to move the testing site to Alaska as a form of penance.

Every time the film opens in that toxic desert, alone in his room, he must have remembered.

THE CROW
1994
DIRECTED BY ALEX PROYAS

Wearing a black leather jacket and boots, with a t-shirt bearing the prophetic phrase 'Hangman's Joke', Brandon Lee was to enter the room carrying a sack of groceries. Inside the bag nestled a generous reservoir of fake blood, and a small explosive charge or squib. When actor Michael Masse discharged his revolver into Lee, the charge would go off and the blood would gush out as if he had been wounded. The tragedy of what happened next has haunted Hollywood ever since, and spawned numerous urban myths.

On the morning of March 31st 1993, filming of *The Crow* was continuing as usual on the premises of Carolco Studios in Wilmington, South Carolina. The mid-budget gothic supernatural drama adapted from the comic book by James O'Barr had only eight days left to complete, and 28-year-old Lee was preparing to marry his fiancée Liza Hutton a week after that.

Unbeknownst to anyone on-set, the .44 calibre handgun intended for the scene was not properly primed and prepared. Several weeks earlier the same gun had been used in a series of close-up shots which involved loading 'dummy' bullets into its chambers. Having no correctly prepared dummy bullets to hand, the props department took real bullets and removed the gunpowder. How one of these bullet tips broke off and lodged in the barrel was never established, though later some witnesses claimed they saw an unsupervised actor playing around with the gun.

The evening before the fatal filming, in order to save money, the production sent the firearms expert home and handed over the task to an inexperienced props assistant. Without checking the barrel for obstructions, he loaded the gun with blanks, which have enough propellant charge to shoot a bullet.

Brandon Lee ignited the squib just as a real bullet pierced his abdomen on his right side. Rushed to the New Hanover Medical centre, he died 12 hours later after doctors failed to staunch the bleeding. The bullet had perforated his stomach and lodged near to his spine.

The actual footage of his fatal shooting was not used in the film, as some have claimed, but was handed over to the Wilmington Police Force during their investigation. It is assumed that Lee's family had it destroyed. The film was completed using some digital trickery and a stand-in.

Brandon Lee was buried next to his father Bruce Lee, who, it is said, foretold his son's death. The sad truth is that he wasn't killed by a curse, or by Hong Kong triads, but by the cost-cutting of the studio, who were sufficiently ashamed of their actions to sell the film on to another company for distribution.

THE DAY THE EARTH STOOD STILL
1951
DIRECTED BY ROBERT WISE

In an extended scene at the end of *The Day The Earth Stood Still*, the pioneering sci-fi film from the early 1950s, the robot Gort prepares to punish humankind after the US army shoots down his alien companion Klaatu.

Patricia Neal's character races to the spaceship to stop him, where she utters the immortal lines 'Klaatu barada nikto' before the robot carries her into the spaceship itself. Little did the audience know the physical cost the sequence was having on the actor playing Gort, who until a few weeks earlier had been employed as a doorman at Grauman's Chinese Theatre on Hollywood Boulevard.

Lock Martin, full name Joseph Lockard Martin Jr, was born in 1916 and measured a full 7 foot 7 inches tall. From the word go the race had been on to find an actor tall enough to fulfil the function of the story; various actors were proposed for the role, with studio chief Darryl F Zanuck suggesting Jack Palance. It wasn't until extremely late in the day that someone remembered a tall member of staff at Grauman's. He was hired. Up until then, Martin had been a nobody, working in many short-term jobs including employment as a cowboy and also as a dairyman.

The Gort costume was a problem for Martin from the outset; although physically tall he was not a strong man. There were two Gort suits, one that zipped up from the front and one that zipped up from the back. They were only made from foam-rubber, but Martin found that wearing a suit for more than half-an-hour was completely exhausting. In the extended scene he has to carry both Patricia Neal and the dead body of Klaatu onto the spaceship (made of wood, wire and plaster-of-paris) up a ramp. Earlier Martin's difficulty in standing on the ramp is concealed by a glowing special effect that covers his lower legs. The only way to get around his inability to carry either actor was using a combination of dummies, trick-shot angles and wires.

Later, in the iconic final scene, with Gort in the background and a revived Klaatu giving a warning to mankind on the ramp of the spaceship, Martin is standing where he is precisely because he can't stand on the ramp at all. If you look closely you can see how the effort is taking its toll; he was experiencing painful muscular spasms by this point, and you can see his right arm twitching.

Martin was almost certainly suffering from Marfan's syndrome, a connective tissue disorder that creates an elongated form. He had a brief career – scenes in *The Incredible Shrinking Man* were deleted, but he was known to a generation of children for hosting a TV show entitled *The Gentle Giant*. He died in 1959, his late career elusive, rumoured to have played the Yeti in Val Guest's *The Abominable Snowman* (1957), but more likely to have played the Yeti in *The Snow Creature* (1954), and an alien in *Invaders from Mars* (1953).

DELIVERANCE
1972
DIRECTED BY JOHN BOORMAN

The male rape scene in *Deliverance* has passed into a kind of legendary place, something to be spoken of in hushed tones. After filming it, actor Ned Beatty found himself an unwilling spokesperson for male rape. Burt Reynolds didn't help matters by insisting that the supposed penetration had actually taken place. And in a curious aside, Stanley Kubrick developed an unhealthy obsession with the actor who utters the immortal line, 'squeal like a pig'.

Director John Boorman tells his experience of the shoot. 'We shot by the edge of the river for three days in a laurel grove; it was about an hour from the hotel in a four-wheel-drive vehicle.' He'd liked the 'lime-green' effect of the leaves, and the twisted branches and carpet of dead leaves on the forest floor all added to the air of menace. This is where the hillbillies finally get to capture the rafting party in a backwater zone; Jon Voight is tied to a laurel tree by the throat as Bill McKinney orders Ned Beatty to strip and the rape takes place.

In the original script Boorman had written in a string of obscenities, 'but Warners wanted us to shoot coverage for TV as well'. Boorman's writing partner Rospo Pallenberg came up with the line just days beforehand, and Boorman liked it so much he kept it in the shooting script. Burt Reynolds in his autobiography described how the two actors got into the role so thoroughly that 'Bill McKinney was actually penetrating poor Ned and he had to go in and drag him off! It was completely untrue, of course'.

It was the beginning of an unpleasant journey for Ned Beatty, a stage actor in his very first film role. 'He actually felt he *had* been raped,' recalls Boorman. In 1989 Beatty wrote a heartfelt editorial for the *New York Times* in which he revealed he had been stigmatised for 20 years as a result of the scene; strangers still call out 'squeal like a pig' to him on the streets.

Boorman does tell one very funny story about the film, and he's not revealed it before. 'When Stanley Kubrick was casting for *Full Metal Jacket* he wanted Bill McKinney to play the Drill Sergeant. Kubrick phoned me up and said, "What's Bill McKinney like?" And I said he's a very good actor and a lovely guy. And Kubrick said [adopting a sceptical tone] "Come on now – that's the most terrifying scene ever put on film

and that guy has gotta be an awful person." He phoned me two or three times about Bill McKinney and eventually offered him the part.'

'Bill told me later that he was in the LA airport about to come to London and he got a message from Kubrick to cancel. He was paid in full but Kubrick couldn't bear to face him – he was just too afraid!'

DON'T LOOK NOW
1973
DIRECTED BY NICOLAS ROEG

It appears regularly on those 'top ten sexy scenes of all time' lists, but the legend of it being improvised, and real, isn't at all accurate.

Donald Sutherland and Julie Christie are the married couple visiting a wintry Venice after the tragic death of their child. Sutherland's character is a whiskery restoration expert working on the crumbling architecture of the city. After a walk along the side of the San Marco Canal they walk into what is called Hotel Europa and go upstairs. They talk, she bathes. A naked Sutherland works on his art and architectural drawings. Finally they have sex. Roeg's technique of intercutting their sex with a later scene of them getting dressed for the evening is justly celebrated – Steven Soderbergh included an homage to it in *Out of Sight*.

Roeg used two locations for the scene. The lobby and exteriors are the Hotel Gabrielli just east of the Piazza San Marco. The actual room where the scene takes place is in the slightly more upmarket Bauer Grunwald on the Campo San Moise. The scene was filmed first thing in the production after torrential rain slowed down the outdoors shoot. Christie was by all accounts nervous, but Roeg followed the standard practice of a reduced film crew to make her more comfortable. The scene proved so convincing that many are convinced the sex was real.

This one piece of warmth in the entire chilly film wasn't improvised as legend has it. Roeg had actually planned the love scene shortly before coming to Venice because he felt the script was too full of arguments between Christie and Sutherland and he wanted something to lighten the mood.

When Sutherland and Christie filmed the bedroom scene, they'd only met for the first time two days earlier. On *The Jonathan Ross Show* in 2008, Sutherland recalled that the scene was anything but sexy to film. It was filmed without a microphone. Using two 'unblimped Arriflexes' the noise from the uncased cameras was deafening, with Roeg directing every move of their bodies.

The music is worth remarking on. While he was already filming in Venice, Roeg bumped into a producer friend named Ugo Mariotti riding on a vaporetto water-taxi. Mariotti was travelling with the

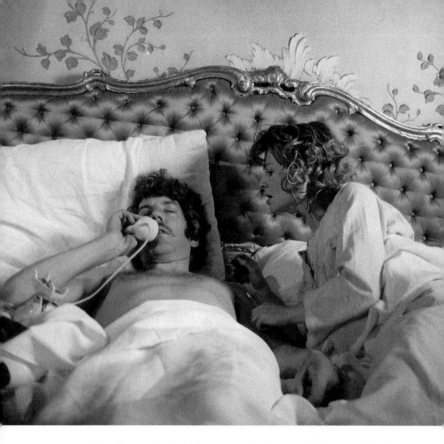

composer Pino Donaggio, best-known at the time for the international hit 'You Don't Have to Say You Love Me'. He was interested in writing for film. Mariotti introduced them.

Roeg was enthralled. Despite resistance from the producers he persisted in believing that their meeting was fated, and wrote the score for the film; as a result Donaggio went on to become a successful film composer – his music for Brian De Palma (*Carrie*, for example) being the best known. The piercing, melancholic flute motif in the love-scene is played by Donaggio himself.

DR NO
1962
DIRECTED BY TERENCE YOUNG

> *"I NEVER THOUGHT I LOOKED SEXY IN THE WHITE BIKINI ... THEY WANTED ME TO WEAR THIS JAMAICA-STYLE ONE, WITH BANANAS AND FLOWERS. SO MY GIRLFRIEND AND I MADE ONE."*
>
> *URSULA ANDRESS*

When Ursula Andress rises like Botticelli's Aphrodite from the turquoise Jamaican sea, wearing a wide-strapped scalloped bikini, cream-coloured, she sets a benchmark for the Bond girls which has never been equalled. But can you guess who made it, and the kind of bikini the producers originally had in mind?

The first entry in the official Bond canon produced by Albert R Broccoli and Harry Saltzman did not, as expected, go with Ian Fleming's first Bond novel. *Casino Royale* had already been shot for TV in 1954, and besides, the two producers did not have the rights for it. As for the role of Bond himself, Cary Grant was too expensive. Curiously the film that got Sean Connery the job was his stint in the forgotten 1959 Disney fantasy *Darby O'Gill and the Little People*.

Ursula Andress is Honey Ryder – a name, not a profession. She's the daughter of a missing marine biologist and she believes the villainous Dr No is responsible for her father's mysterious fate. Bond, just woken on the beach of Crab Keys, watches her knife-wielding arrival accompanied by cod-Jamaican pop. Is this saturnine loafer stealing her shells? She can only dream.

Andress is Swiss-German and spent many of her formative years in the torrid business of Italian farce. At the time of *Dr No* she was married to one Peter Derek – later the husband of the more famous Bo. Despite some years in the US, her heavy accent remained stubbornly in place, and it's a surprise to discover her voice is dubbed throughout – the *Schweizerdeutsch* replaced by the dulcet tones of Monica Van der Zyl (who was later to voice-coach Gert Fröbe for his villainous role in *Goldfinger*).

In a Christies sale in February 2001, the *Dr No* bikini netted £41,000 when it was bought by the owner of Planet Hollywood. The actress still had it in her possession, and had found it tucked away in her attic in Rome. Though admitting she pretty much owed her career to the most famous 'bikini moment in film history', according to one recent poll, she had never much cared for it.

'I never thought I looked sexy in the white bikini,' Andress said years later. In another interview she called it 'lousy'. And the reason she can criticise? 'I had to make it myself,' she told Canada's *Toronto Star* in March 2009. 'They wanted me to wear this Jamaican-style one, with bananas and flowers. So my girlfriend and I made one in Jamaica out of this beige material.'

EASY RIDER
1969
DIRECTED BY DENNIS HOPPER

It was the film that defined a generation – a fizzingly original, chaotic counter-culture classic that shook up Hollywood, launched the career of Jack Nicholson and created a feud between its stars Peter Fonda and Dennis Hopper that remains unresolved to this day. But *Easy Rider* is probably best known as the first film that depicted drug-use without the usual Hollywood framework of overt disapproval; this was a film that reflected the casual drug-use of many young Americans at the time of the 'Summer of Love'. One scene in particular become famous for its powerful depiction of an LSD trip.

After scoring a big cocaine sale to an LA drugs dealer played by Phil Spector, Peter Fonda and Dennis Hopper take to the road on their big Harley choppers (the loot hidden in the petrol tank), intending to make it to Louisiana for the Mardi Gras. On the way they are harassed by various cops and rednecks (in an Oscar-nominated role Jack Nicholson is the unconventional lawyer who gets them out of jail). When they arrive in New Orleans they go to a brothel, pick up two hookers and go to a cemetery – where they all drop acid and experience a jarring series of unsettling perceptive disorientations and frazzled visions of mortality.

Whereas most of the film was shot by Laszlo Kovacs, the Mardi Gras and cemetery scenes were filmed by Dennis Hopper using a hastily assembled crew and a lowly 16mm camera (Hopper had got the dates of the carnival wrong and had to do this at the last minute) on a $40,000 budget. The sprawling and genuinely drug-fuelled excesses of this particular part of the shoot give the scene an air of particular authenticity.

It seems that the crew were outraged at Hopper's increasingly bizarre behaviour in New Orleans, and many of them had quit by the time they came to film in the cemetery. Famously, Hopper manically tried to get Fonda to talk to the statue of the Madonna as if he were addressing Hopper's own mother, who had committed suicide. And the two hookers who accompany them? They are Toni Basil – a noted choreographer who sang the irritating 1980s pop hit *Mickey* – and Karen Black, who some years later received an Oscar nomination for her waitress role in *Five Easy Pieces*.

The film went on to make millions. Dennis Hopper was paid $1 million to film the experimental and entirely forgotten homage to Godard called *The Last Movie*, before retiring to live in DH Lawrence's house in New Mexico – with a drug habit rumoured to have approached three grams of cocaine a day, according to Peter Biskind in *Easy Riders, Raging Bulls*. Fonda too seemed to vanish after directing *The Hired Hand* and never wholly resolved a feud with Hopper over royalties. Latterly he appeared as Mephisto in that slightly less well-received motorbike movie, *Ghost Rider*.

ELEPHANT MAN
1980
DIRECTED BY DAVID LYNCH

Nurse Nora is approaching the isolation ward of the London Hospital with a breakfast tray for the special new patient. This patient is the so-called Elephant Man and the film is about to reveal his full deformity for the first time. Her scream and the crash of the tray carries all the way downstairs to the office of the hospital governor, played by John Gielgud, who is with the surgeon Treves, played by Anthony Hopkins. What were the reasons behind the film's long delay in showing the full horror of the Elephant Man?

Joseph (called John in the film) Merrick suffered from a rare disease now thought to be the Proteus Syndrome. He was born in 1862 and by the age of 12 was peddling shoe-polish on the streets, rejected by his own mother. His face and body were covered in bone-like growths which created an extreme and (to the casual onlooker) alarming appearance. With no means to earn a living, Merrick became a reluctant star attraction on a travelling freak show.

In reality Merrick was always treated with 'the greatest kindness' by the show owners – though for dramatic reasons Lynch chose to portray this period of his life as especially painful and distressing. As the years went by, Merrick was taken up as a special cause by the surgeon Frederick Treves, an anatomist later knighted for performing an appendectomy on Edward VII. In the late 1880s Merrick became a celebrity, thanks mainly to the ministrations of Treves; the public was fascinated by this monster with the soul of a poet.

Lynch's much-discussed technique of delaying the first glimpse of Merrick was born out of a disaster that, he claims, nearly drove him to suicide. Lynch had tried to develop his own formulation for the celebrated make-up that covers John Hurt's face – in, of all things, a garage in Wembley. But a mere ten days before the shoot it became clear that his efforts had failed. 'It was like concrete,' Lynch recalled later. 'There was no way John could move in that thing.' Production supervisor Terry Clegg also remembers it vividly. 'It was rather like someone wearing a pair of long-johns covered in rubber latex – a disaster.'

In great haste, make-up specialist Chris Tucker was flown in from America, immediately increasing the film's budget by some 25 per

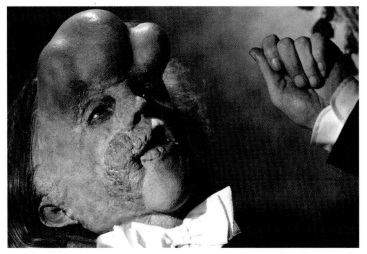

cent. As Lynch filmed with stand-ins, Tucker developed Merrick's face from scratch, using actual plaster casts of the man's head that had been made on his death, aged 27.

Later Lynch decided he liked the slow revelation of Merrick's deformity, and he manipulated the final edit to heighten this effect. 'I felt that [otherwise] people would start looking at it too much as a horror film,' he explained.

Chris Tucker's last-minute make-up job became celebrated in Hollywood circles, and the year after *Elephant Man* was released the Academy of Motion Pictures came up with a special new category for Best Make-Up entirely as a result.

THE ENIGMA OF KASPAR HAUSER
1974
DIRECTED BY WERNER HERZOG

On May 26th 1828, a strangely behaved teenaged boy appeared on the streets of Nürnberg in Germany. He was taken into the care of the local jailer when it became apparent that he had the mental development of a six year old and was unable to communicate in the most basic of ways. He had no concept of the world outside his cell and was bizarrely sensitive to magnets and metal. The boy, named Kaspar Hauser, became a celebrity after a connection to the Dukes of Baden was rumoured.

German film director Werner Herzog was drawn to the story for its themes of alienation and disassociation. After a series of landscape shots which begin the movie, Herzog shows Hauser in a gloomy cell, his legs chained to the floor, playing with a toy horse and in no obvious distress. Church bells ring outside. He's dressed in dirty clothes and eats his bread and drinks his water with some relish. Then a man comes and drags him outside.

The actor playing Hauser, whose full name still remains unknown to the general public, is Bruno S. His past resembles Kaspar Hauser's in a remarkable number of ways. A few days after Herzog had finished his script he happened to be watching a documentary on German TV made by a student filmmaker named Lutz Eisholz. On it he saw Bruno S working as a street singer and immediately became convinced that this was the man to play his lead.

He arranged to meet Bruno S via Eisholz after being told that Bruno didn't take kindly to strangers. In fact they got on famously. He was also startled to discover that Bruno had been incarcerated for most of his life, after being beaten up by his prostitute mother, which robbed him of the power of speech from the ages of three to seven. Sent first to a special school and then to an actual asylum, one day he was released without warning, just as Hauser is in this scene.

Filming in the walled Bavarian town of Dinkelsbühl was a challenging experience, since the eccentricity of the actor never really settled down. 'Sometimes during shooting we had to stop because Bruno wanted to talk about his pain and his catastrophes – and I really insisted that the crew would focus, listen and be kind,' recalls Herzog. Though nearly 41 at the time, Bruno was playing a teenager.

Herzog went on to make one more film with Bruno S, but he's been seen little since. Herzog has always mocked those who insisted that Hauser was of royal blood, but after several DNA tests, the most recent held in 2002, a 95 per cent match with the descendants of Stephanie de Beauharnais (the Grand Duchess of Baden) seems to have been established. The real Hauser was assassinated in mysterious circumstances aged only 21.

THE EXORCIST
1973
DIRECTED BY WILLIAM FRIEDKIN

Max Von Sydow arrives outside the house at 3600 Prospect Avenue, close to the Potomac River in Georgetown. It is an iconic moment in modern cinema. Father Merrin, the Exorcist of the title, steps out of a cab into the cold night-time fog and looks up at the bedroom window of the possessed little girl. An eerie shaft of light illuminates part of the scene; the priest is thin, ominous even, in the darkness. In the bedroom the child Regan – possessed by the Devil – senses the arrival of an old enemy.

Played by Linda Blair, Regan is caked in convincing-looking vomit made from dried split-peas and oatmeal. Her lips are cracked and her skin flaky and inflamed. Her eyes are unearthly and feral. She is tied down to a hefty wooden bed: we have already seen it jump around the room in earlier scenes with another priest. This piece of special effects kit, it would later transpire, caused serious back injuries both to Blair and to the actress who played her mother, Ellen Burstyn.

Director William Friedkin had turned the bedroom into a giant refrigerator with a bank of air-conditioners. It was yet another item in the long list of grievances later levelled at the director, who favoured extreme filming scenarios to get the actorly responses he required. As Father Merrin begins to intone his prayers, Regan hurls foul-mouthed insults at him in a gravelly voice produced by the swallowing and regurgitating of pulpy eggs. Doors slam. The bed leaps. Vomit drools. Then the *coup de grâce*: the 360-degree turn of the head. The sound you hear is of a special effects man twisting an old leather wallet. The dummy that makes the famous head-twisting movement was conceived by special effects wizard Dick Smith.

Friedkin enjoyed spreading the story that the movie was cursed. It's commonly mentioned that Linda Blair claimed that *The Exorcist* ruined her life, though writer and critic Mark Kemode doubts she ever said it. Certainly her happiness deteriorated as she got older, ending up with a drugs conviction in 1977 (where the ruin was more explicitly of her own making). Though nominated for an Oscar for *The Exorcist* she didn't win (by common consent) after it emerged that Friedkin had been far from frank about the role of her body doubles. One of them,

Eileen Dietz, sued the production. Another stand-in – a contortionist named Linda R Hager – solely performed the infamous 'spider' scene that made it into a recent version of the film.

Exorcist is routinely held up as the scariest film of all time, but all four sequels/prequels have performed poorly. The author of the original novel, William Peter Blatty, has always maintained that the tale was based on a true story that took place in a suburban Maryland home in 1949, though the child in question was a 13-year-old boy. This was dramatised in the TV film *Possessed* (2000).

THE FOUR FEATHERS
1939
DIRECTED BY ZOLTAN KORDA

When the Korda brothers came to shoot the climactic Battle of Omdurman scene for *The Four Feathers*, there were more than a few relics left over from the original battle exactly 40 years earlier. But who was the old man who kept ruining the shot as the Dervishes (or Ansar, as they are now called) charged the British Army?

The Four Feathers had already been made three times before the *émigré* Korda brothers came to this version with Ralph Richardson. It was a movie completely of its time – a stirring colonial epic of derring-do and an officer who has been accused of cowardice and must clear his name. Set in the foment of late 19th-century Sudan, this version of AEW Mason's novel moved the Battle of Omdurman firmly centre stage.

With Zoltan Korda directing, Alexander Korda producing and Vincent Korda designing the production, one of the great powerhouse teams of 1930s British cinema was at the helm. The brothers were determined to use their recently licensed Technicolor process to maximum effect. They hired Col WF Stirling (chief of staff to Lawrence of Arabia) to oversee the military details, but almost immediately factual accuracy had to go out of the window when Alexander Korda didn't want to use blue uniforms in one scene because this would interfere with his vision of Technicolor.

In effect, the filmmakers became the guests of the British Army for the duration of the film. They also authorised the use on film of a large contingent of the Sudan Defence Force Mounted Infantry. For the Dervishes, the production brought in several hundred Hadendowa from the Red Sea Hills by railway; the Hadendowa insisted on using real kaskara swords in the filming, much to the alarm of the rest of the crew.

In effect, the Kordas were re-creating the actual battle, with more or less the same components and the same foes in the same place. In one account even the uniforms the 17th Lancers are wearing were authentic – found in some backroom at a Cairo army base.

So it was no surprise that feelings were rising high at certain points in the shooting of the battle scene; Korda had ordered the extras to charge forward at the British Army and then die on cue under a hail of bullets. All the extras did so apart from one man in his

late 60s, who resolutely refused to play dead, and therefore ruined every shot.

The reason? Through interpreters the man made his feelings known. He had fought in the original battle of Omdurman and had survived. He was damned if he was going to die at British hands now – even fictitiously.

GLADIATOR
2000
DIRECTED BY RIDLEY SCOTT

The death of actor Oliver Reed during the filming of *Gladiator* proved a dilemma for director Ridley Scott and producer Douglas Wick. The choice was a stark one: call in the insurance, or rewrite the script and with a little computer trickery re-create the actor digitally for his final scene – the moment of his death, as it happened. They decided on the latter course.

Set in the Roman Empire around the year 180 AD, *Gladiator* is the story of a general named Maximus, played by Russell Crowe. It begins with an extended battle scene and moves swiftly to the death of the emperor Marcus Aurelius (played by Richard Harris) and an effective *coup* staged by his son Commodus (a simpering Joaquin Phoenix), who moves rapidly to destroy the power of Maximus. Maximus, stripped of all his wealth and power, his family assassinated, is sold into slavery and sent to the African gladiatorial training camp of Proximo (Oliver Reed).

Reed is the slave-owner who trains up his latest star for shows at the Coliseum in Rome. He has many of the best lines in the movie. One afternoon, after Reed had completed roughly 90 per cent of his role, he suffered a heart attack at 'The Pub' at 136 Archbishop Street in Valletta, Malta. He had polished off three bottles of rum and had been arm-wrestling with five British sailors from HMS Cumberland. Some years earlier he had predicted that he would die 'in a bar of a heart attack – full of laughter'.

In order to finish off the scenes where the tables are turned on the enemies of Maximus, where Proximo looks up before he is killed and says 'shadows and dust', Scott had to comb through all the out-takes and previous scenes to find something useful. He then hired a body double and scanned Reed's face onto him using several complex CGI techniques; his actual words 'shadows and dust' are in fact re-used from another scene, where Maximus is about to fight fellow gladiator Tigris. Somewhat ironically the scene cost exactly the same to make – $3 million – as a previously rejected episode where Maximus was to fight a CGI-generated rhino in the Coliseum.

In an extra on the DVD entitled *Shadows and Dust: Resurrecting Proximo*, editor Pietro Scalia gives a detailed account of this process

of bringing Oliver Reed back from the grave to complete his final scene. Brandon Lee had been given similar treatment in *The Crow* in 1994, after his accidental death during filming. It remains to be seen whether the technology can improve to such an extent that abandoned films such as *Dark Blood* – River Phoenix's last film – can be recovered with so few of the scenes completed.

THE GODFATHER
1972
DIRECTED BY FRANCIS FORD COPPOLA

About 50 minutes into *The Godfather*, just after the 'sleeps with the fishes' scene, Mafia henchmen Clemenza and Rocco get into a car with Paulie. They intend to kill him. Clemenza, played by Richard S Castellano, claims that they are going to look for 'mattresses' (safe houses) and directs Paulie to drive to '309 West 43rd street'.

The remarks about 'cannoli' that begin and end the scene have become as famous as anything in *The Godfather*, and have been incorporated into the whole lore surrounding US Italian-American Mafiosi movies. Clemenza's preoccupation with the ricotta-filled Sicilian pastries initiates a food theme that has informed every gangster drama since, from *Goodfellas* to *The Sopranos*.

Francis Ford Coppola had a good deal of trouble making *The Godfather*, but he made a fine call in securing the Bronx-born actor Richard S Castellano. Strange to relate, Castellano was one of the best-paid actors in the entire movie (he had received a Best Supporting Actor Oscar nomination at the 43rd Academy Awards, and was briefly very hot property).

The scene where Paulie gets popped begins with Clemenza leaving his house and his wife shouting 'don't forget the cannoli' – a last-minute addition to the dialogue made by Coppola on the day. Initially you see two children in a toy car, riding down the drive in front of the parked car. Coppola has said these children are 'Augie and Francie' – that is, his brother and himself, who were about that age at the timeframe in which the movie is set (just after WWII).

There follows a montage of stock footage of New York at the period, and then a shot of the car driving in the countryside beyond New York. Clemenza asks to pull over to 'take a leak'. It's a wintry scene. In the distance shimmers The Statue of Liberty. As Clemenza stands outside, three shots are fired by Rocco in the car into Paulie's head. Clemenza walks back to the car and says, as Rocco hurries to get out, 'leave the gun – take the cannoli'. Carefully he takes possession of the wrapped white package as Paulie lies dead against the steering wheel. Coppola gave all credit to the actor in later years. 'Richie improvised the line,' he said.

But why did Castellano never appear in *The Godfather II*? Fans were baffled by the scene in which Fredo mentions Clemenza's heart attack and points to Frankie Five Angels wearing a black armband in remembrance.

It seems that Castellano had not only asked for too much money, but had also demanded that his future wife Ardell Sheridan (who asks him to get the cannoli in the first film) write his lines. It was a request too far for Coppola, who insists nonethless that he wanted Castellano right up to the last minute.

Castellano died of a heart attack in 1988 – aged only 55.

THE GRADUATE
1967
DIRECTED BY MIKE NICHOLS

Anne Bancroft never escaped her role as the middle-aged seductress of *The Graduate*. She wasn't even middle-aged when she did it. Dustin Hoffman, in contrast, performing admirably in his début role and, cast as the unlikely source of her sexual attentions, went on to have a career of incredible depth and variety. Anne Bancroft was always Mrs Robinson.

In one of the most famous scenes in the film (and this is a film with several famous scenes, famous poster images and famous lines) Dustin Hoffman's character Benjamin is helping Anne Bancroft's Mrs Robinson to undress. She is sitting. He is standing. He reaches over and grabs her right breast. He then turns his head away from the camera, walks over to the wall of the hotel room and bangs his head against it.

This has always been considered a masterful expression of Benjamin's self-doubt and anxiety. He's seducing Mrs Robinson, for heaven's sake. She's an old family friend. It's a bit like sleeping with his mother. He really doesn't know how this is going to pan out and the dread is creeping in. He's thinking of stopping it all right now and leaving.

In fact Dustin's Hoffman's breast-grab was impromptu and unscripted. He had planned it beforehand, he later explained, to imitate the kind of embarrassed fumblings of a school-boy with an inappropriate physical lunge. The reason Benjamin turns round and goes to the wall was actually because Hoffman was laughing; his clumsy sexual foray was met with a hearty guffaw from director Mike Nichols standing behind the camera. Rather than finish the scene and lose the moment, Dustin, from the beginning a consummate professional, hid his laughter and carried on. The scene was later post-dubbed.

At the time, Anne Bancroft was already married to actor and comedian Mel Brooks in what was to prove one of the most successful marriages in Hollywood before her death in 2005. By coincidence Dustin Hoffman was set to play a role in Mel Brooks's *The Producers* the following year, and Brooks gave him permission to audition for *The Graduate* simply because he never believed that Hoffman had the looks to be cast as the object of his wife's attentions. He couldn't have been more wrong.

Though she was always busy, Bancroft never again reached the dizzy heights of *The Graduate*. To make matters worse, the legs on the iconic poster advertising the film weren't even hers (they belonged to Linda Gray, later of *Dallas*, then unknown). She was in fact only six years older than Hoffman, and eight years older than her onscreen daughter; make-up was used to age her. With the cruelty of Hollywood towards the sight of female middle-ageing, Bancroft endured an early eclipse of her career.

Everyone thought she was older than she really was.

THE GREAT ESCAPE
1963
DIRECTED BY JOHN STURGES

Steve McQueen had a thing about speed. He loved bikes and fast cars. It's said that the asbestos suit he used on the semi-professional racing circuit (and while making films like *Le Mans*) caused the cancer that killed him before the fast cars did. In *The Great Escape* the script called for his character to escape the WWII German POW camp by catching a train. McQueen wasn't having it and personally pitched the famous motorcycle chase scene to director John Sturges.

Filming began on location near Munich in the summer of 1962, with a script written by James Clavell, who had himself been imprisoned in a Japanese POW camp. Some of the original escapees were hired as technical advisers, including F/Lt Wally Floody, a Canadian mining engineer and wartime Spitfire pilot who had been responsible for the tunnel traps and their camouflage. Many of the film's characters are amalgams of real people, but it's thought that most of McQueen's Virgil Hilts actually comes from a Brit – F/Lt Barry Mahon of 121 Squadron RAF, to be precise, who was also present on set and to whom McQueen took quite a shine, incorporating elements of his story into the script.

McQueen's character is the most charismatic in the movie – the 'Cooler King' whose insolence and individualism probably owed more to Kerouac than to 1940s pluck. There was much of McQueen in Virgil Hilts, and it was no surprise that he reacted badly when informed that insurance precluded him doing the stunt himself. 'I could have bust my melon,' he fumed before handing over his on-screen duties to Bud Ekins, his Californian friend and stunt double who with a little hair dye made a passable McQueen. The eventual leap over the wire fence into Switzerland is safer than it looks – the fence is made out of string and rubber.

There was one more problem to be solved – in the long chase scene beforehand, in which McQueen really does ride a motorcycle. McQueen kept out-running the stuntmen dressed as German soldiers sent in pursuit. Once again he came up with the solution: he himself would play the Germans, and so he does. With a nifty piece of editing, what you see is actually McQueen chasing himself. The machines are 1961 British 650cc Triumphs, mocked-up in German colours.

McQueen's speeding activities weren't confined to the set, either. During the weeks of filming he picked up 37 speeding fines and wrapped his Mercedes 300-SL round a tree one day on his way to work.

HEAVEN'S GATE
1980
DIRECTED BY MICHAEL CIMINO

Christ Church College in Oxford, most recently seen as a handsome backdrop for The Golden Compass, features prominently in the opening scene of the Hollywood western Heaven's Gate. It's an unlikely location, and it isn't even supposed to be Oxford. Up against the clock and already sensing that the movie was in trouble, Michael Cimino found himself having to shoot the beginning of his western illegally in the streets of Oxford.

The film has gone down in history as an exalted directorial folly that bankrupted United Artists. Its completely out-of-control director spent the then astronomical sum of $40 million on its production, a sum he racked up with a blizzard of unnecessary spending (hand-made cowboy hats and transporting a steam train on a flatbed across several states, for example).

In England, Cimino had belatedly found the prudence so lacking in the rest of the movie – a film even now a Hollywood byword for ruinous excess. According to Steven Bach's *Final Cut*, the opening scene was shot after principal photography had ceased on a special new budget of $3 million. For the first time in the entire production, Cimino stuck rigidly to his budget and to his five-day shooting schedule.

The opening caption may say 'Harvard College, Cambridge, Massachusetts, 1870' but Kris Kristofferson is running through an archway in Oxford thousands of miles away. A scene-setter shows about 20 minutes of a college graduation ceremony. Cimino was only in England because Harvard itself had denied filming rights.

Everything went as planned for four days, until Cimino discovered that the Oxford authorities had denied him the right to shoot on a Sunday. Realising he still didn't have a critical shot of the sun rising behind a clock-tower, and having no possibility of finding extra money, Cimino took matters into his own hands.

After secret preparations, which included 'persuasion' of the college guards to look the other way, just after midnight on Saturday evening earth was poured over an entire asphalt street and 60 feet of dolly tracks were laid. Cimino 'stole' the shot at dawn in three takes, and everything was cleared away by 8 a.m. after the production had wrapped.

A few months later, Cimino delivered a five-hour cut to the studio. Despite a reputation gained as the director of *The Deer Hunter*, his subsequent career proved a succession of diminishing returns, and erosion of studio trust in his abilities, although many have since made the case for *Heaven's Gate* as a lost masterpiece. A 219-minute cut released in the 1980s is held up as the beginning of the director's cut phenomenon – so in a further irony, Cimino was indirectly responsible for this highly lucrative new form of reselling the same movie over and over again.

HIGH NOON
1952
DIRECTED BY FRED ZINNEMANN

It's minutes to high noon. In a famous montage, the cowardly towns-folk of Hadleyville, New Mexico, have left the streets; they wait guiltily in saloon bars, chapels and their private homes. The music of the soundtrack wells. The clocks tick, inexorably. Marshal Will Kane, played by Gary Cooper, is in his office, writing out a letter 'to be opened in the event of my death'. Frank Miller is coming to Hadleyville, and he's going to shoot the Marshal. The steam of the train is turning black as it approaches the station. Three gunmen wait to greet him.

Often described as an 'existential western' and a named favourite film of Bill Clinton's, *High Noon* was made on a budget of $750,000 and filmed in only 28 days. Most of it was shot in the Columbia back-lot at Burbank, where director Frank Zinnemann and cinematographer Floyd Crosby used the LA smog to make the sky look blindingly white in contrast to Kane's black clothes. *High Noon* did not look like a conventional sagebrush western. This is in part thanks to its marked political inflection, variously read as pro and anti Senator McCarthy, whose purges were then convulsing Hollywood. It usually read as liberal in essence. Arch-Republican John Wayne criticised the script as un-American but then told Cooper, while presenting him with an Oscar, that he wished he could find a role as good for himself.

Gary Cooper won a second Oscar for his performance in *High Noon*. Cooper's career in the western genre lasted 35 years, as long as the wild west lasted in reality, but he was not the first choice for the film (Marlon Brando, Montgomery Clift – the list is long). Aged 51 he was haggard and ill; during the shoot he was plagued with a bleeding stomach ulcer and chronic lower back and hip problems. That gaunt, worn face is a face of genuine illness and pain, and many of the short takes of him were short by necessity.

One of the earliest moving images in cinema history was of a train speeding towards the camera, and it was to Jamestown that Zinnemann took his crew to get this shot. As the noonday train speeds towards the town, bearing the man who intends to shoot Kane, Zinnemann and Crosby lie on the tracks as the crew wait a few hundred yards away. What they didn't realise was that the change

from white to black smoke was an indication that the brakes on the train had failed. Both stumbled to safety only just in time – but the tripod of the camera snagged on the rails and the camera was smashed by the train.

Miraculously, the film footage survived, and is used in the movie.

IN THE HEAT OF THE NIGHT
1967
DIRECTED BY NORMAN JEWISON

It's been called one of the most revolutionary acts committed to film. Forty-odd years after the event it still packs a punch; note that one of the main characters in this scene is a pioneering African-American and the other, an autocratic white plantation owner, looks like Dick Cheney.

In 1965, observed Mark Harris in *Slate Magazine*, the Hollywood landscape was such that, in order to get the film made, producer Walter Mirisch had to run the numbers 'and show United Artists that a picture in which Sidney Poitier one-upped a town full of white rubes could make money, even if it never opened in a single Southern city'.

Sidney Poitier plays the Philadelphia detective visiting a relative in the Deep South. He's arrested, vexatiously, by the local police, and there begins an almost routine process of trying to fix him up for a local murder. In a performance that won him an Oscar, Rod Steiger plays the role of Police Chief Bill Gilliespie; initially an oafish redneck, the growing respect between himself and Poitier's Detective Virgil Tibbs is one of the great two-handers of cinema.

When production began in 1966, Poitier refused to shoot in the South. He was still traumatised by the experience of being tailed by Klansmen when visiting North Carolina with Harry Belafonte. Only recently a burning cross had been planted on the lawn of his wife's home in Pleasantville. Under pressure, Poitier reluctantly agreed to a few days of tense location work in Tennessee. Plagued by whooping rednecks, much like a scene from the film itself, Poitier told Jewison that he slept with a gun under his pillow. So it was in Illinois, not Mississippi, that the majority of the film was made.

The scene in question takes place in an orchid house attached to a grand mansion. Wealthy local Eric Endicott is being questioned about the murder by Detective Tibbs. He doesn't like it. He's not used to being 'talked back to' by a black man. Tibbs speaks calmly, politely. Endicott lunges towards him, past a large white orchid in full bloom, and slaps him on his face for his insolence. Without warning, Tibbs slaps him back, harder. Endicott, astonished, nearly falls over. 'There was a time,' he tells Tibbs, 'when I could have had you shot.' Tibbs, Gillespie and an astonished black servant bearing glasses of lemonade depart the room, leaving Endicott to weep.

The slap was not in the script; no-one knew that Poitier was going to do it. And when he does, you feel his reply to every policeman who ever harried him and every humiliation he received over the years. The world changed with that one slap.

THE ITALIAN JOB
1969
DIRECTED BY PETER COLLINSON

The gold bullion has been loaded into the three red, white and blue Mini Coopers at the Museo Egizio. Then follows the police chase through the elegant streets of Turin, plucky manoeuvrable Minis bumping down stone steps, powering through the River Po, revving across factory roofs and wheeling down storm drains. Having shaken the police and the Mafia, the three minis drive onto an adapted coach as we career towards the famous literalism of the cliffhanging ending. But how close did the 'longest commercial for a car ever made' (as director of photography Douglas Slocombe describes the film) come to abandoning the use of Minis altogether? And why do you never see Michael Caine ('you're only supposed to blow the bloody doors off') behind the wheel?

When producer Michael Deeley first approached the British Motor Corporation – the precursor of British Leyland, who made the Minis in those days – he was expecting an enthusiastic response. Instead he recalls that they were 'completely uninterested' and eventually, grudgingly sold the production six cars at trade price. At the same time canny Fiat boss Gianni Agnelli heard about the problems with BMC and immediately offered the production £50,000 in cash plus the use of an unlimited number of Fiat 500s to replace the Minis.

Still, Fiat managed one way or another to be in the movie, with dozens of Cinquecentos onscreen and the Fiat grounds north of Turin forming part of the chase scene. That jump between roofs, for example, is actually at the Fiat factory (Fiat workers by all accounts crossed themselves as they watched the stunt being done).

Lead driver Rémy Julienne, who it's said could make a Mini sit up and beg at traffic lights before whizzing off, was the man who dreamed up the dazzling choreography of these interweaving cars doing things people had never seen cars do before. To keep up the 'patriotic plucky Briton versus Eurotrash' theme of the movie, the cars are nearly always, except for one brief moment, arranged in a red, white and blue formation.

The final part of the scene, with the bullion-laden bus precariously perched on the edge of a cliff in the Swiss-Italian alps, originally had multiple endings. The downdraft of the helicopter nearly blew the bus over before filming had finished, and there was trouble too with the locals using the road; it was the sole approach to a popular restaurant. Michael Caine later said that his plan to resolve the situation (never revealed in the film) was to let the engine run, burn the petrol and restore the equilibrium of the bus.

And why do we never see Michael Caine behind the wheel in one of the most famous car-themed movies of all time? He had never learned to drive.

JAWS
1975
DIRECTED BY STEVEN SPIELBERG

It's one of the best-known 'scream' shots in cinematic history.

Marine biologist Richard Dreyfuss has been sequestered by the police chief of Amity, Long Island (played by Roy Scheider) to investigate a series of shark attacks on local holidaymakers while summer bathing. A reluctant Scheider joins Dreyfuss on his high-tech boat for a night-time survey of the coastal waters, and Dreyfuss scuba-dives into the sea when they come across a wreck of a fishing boat which appears to have been attacked. Dreyfuss prises a huge serrated tooth from the hull of the semi-submerged boat; as he does so the pale face of a corpse floats up from the dark interior and emerges suddenly into full view.

The shark itself only appears 82 minutes into the film, in part thanks to the extensive mechanical problems Spielberg was having with the three versions of his 1.5-ton animatronic creature. They were collectively called Bruce (Spielberg's little joke – it was the name of his lawyer) and required 13 people to operate them. One model was a shark on the end of a 300ft tow line; the second was the left side of the shark; and the third was the right side manipulated via an elaborate 12ft steel rig on an underwater platform. Corrosion and breakages meant that these expensive stars had to be repaired, dried and repainted every evening, much like the helicopters in *Apocalypse Now*.

Spielberg partly chose the location of Martha's Vineyard, Massachusetts to stand in for Long Island because of the requirements of the mechanical sharks; the water there remains shallow up to 12 miles out to sea. The live shark footage he incorporated was filmed in Australia, in truth much more prone to Jaws-style shark attacks than the US coastline (Benchley's original book is loosely based on real-life events from 1916, when a shark killed four people in New Jersey).

As a result of his problems with the model sharks, Spielberg had to rely on his own imagination and some rather old-fashioned directorial skills to suggest menace and threat – hence the use of the camera as the eyes of the shark and John Williams's chugging 'shark theme'.

Filming ended on September 15th 1974; it had taken five and a half months and nerves were fried. Spielberg went on a legendary drinking bender in a Boston hotel and suffered a pronounced anxiety attack.

Months later, after trying out an early edit on a test audience, Spielberg still wasn't happy with the shock of the dead face emerging from the gloom. He wanted the public to 'scream louder'. He asked David Brown and Richard Zanuck for money to re-shoot the scene, and when they refused, he stumped up $100,000 of his own money to film it in the swimming pool belonging to the film's editor Verna Fields. Carnation milk was used to get the murky look of the water.

The audience did scream louder when it was screened again.

LAWRENCE OF ARABIA
1962
DIRECTED BY DAVID LEAN

> *"WHAT THE COSTUME PEOPLE DID ... WAS GRADUALLY CHANGE THE TEXTURE OF THE MATERIAL FROM WHICH [PETER O'TOOLE'S] ARAB CLOTHES WERE MADE ... UNTIL IT WAS JUST MUSLIN, AND AT THE END IT LOOKED ALMOST GHOSTLIKE."*
>
> *DAVID LEAN*

David Lean was a director who obsessively storyboarded and mapped out his films before setting out to shoot them – but one key moment in *Lawrence of Arabia* has a small unscripted improvisation by Peter O'Toole that delighted the director when it emerged spontaneously during a key scene.

Lawrence of Arabia remains one of the great masterpieces of British cinema; its sweeping visual grandeur and heroic wartime individualism is often name-checked by Steven Spielberg as an influence. The film is based on the autobiographical account of TE Lawrence, *The Seven Pillars of Wisdom* (his appalled family refused Sam Spiegel the rights to use the title after viewing the film) and set during WWI. Lean had wanted to cast Albert Finney in the title role, and although Finney agreed to shoot a lengthy screen-test, he later walked away from the project. Instead the thin frame, golden hair and piercing blue eyes of Irishman Peter O'Toole were to be indelibly associated with the image of the maverick English officer who became a key instigator of the Arab revolt against their Ottoman overlords, thus destabilising the region to the benefit of the British war effort.

After being sent off into the desert to find King Feisal of the Hashemites, there's an important moment in the film where Lawrence first dons the famous white robes – he's going native. At first O'Toole slipped on the Arab clothing as per the script, but Lean felt immediately that there was something missing. 'What would you

think a young man would do alone in the desert if he'd just been given these beautiful robes,' he quizzed the actor. O'Toole, realising that a mirror was required but none was in the tent, pulled out his dagger and peered at his reflection in the polished blade. 'Clever boy!' exclaimed the director, who not only used the shot, but repeated it again later in the film, during a celebrated massacre sequence when a column of retreating Turkish soldiers are savagely mown down.

There's one final interesting point to make about this costuming scene. Many years later, Lean was to reveal a trick that progresses over the film's length. When Lawrence first dons his desert robes it symbolises the erosion of his patrician Britishness. But why is it exactly that O'Toole seems so, well, ethereal by the end? 'What the costume people did,' admitted Lean, 'was gradually change the texture of the material from which his Arab clothes were made and they made it thinner until it was just muslin, and at the end it looked almost ghostlike.'

It's a brilliant visual tweak that shows just how important costume can be, and how careful attention to it can manipulate an audience. It's said that O'Toole felt foolish and embarrassed in his flowing garb – but it made him a star.

LIFE OF BRIAN
1979
DIRECTED BY TERRY JONES

During the filming of *Monty Python and the Holy Grail*, Eric Idle liked to tease the press with entirely false descriptions of their next film project – to be called *Jesus Christ: Lust for Glory*. In a rare example of an off-hand comment that became one of the most celebrated comedies ever made, the Pythons soon found themselves in the Caribbean writing the script for their Jesus film, and equally soon found themselves mired in problems with EMI, who withdrew finance in horror at the blasphemous content. But luckily a cameo was at hand.

You can see George Harrison in the scene where a very officious John Cleese, always brilliant as the aggressive jobsworth, is marshalling Graham Chapman through the hysterical throng of the petitioning sick. Graham Chapman has mistakenly been identified as the Messiah, and try as he might, he can't get anyone to believe him. 'Now don't jostle the chosen one, please,' pipes up Michael Palin. 'Don't push that baby in the Saviour's face!' exclaims Cleese in his character-istic strangulated tones. As Chapman squeezes through the crowd, a bearded man in a dark-red headdress (and looking uncannily like Johnny Depp in *Pirates of the Caribbean*) is introduced to him as 'the gentleman who's letting us have the Mount on Saturday'. Scripted as Mr Papadopolous, this is none other than ex-Beatle George Harrison.

It's possibly the most expensive cameo in history – £4 million to be exact. When EMI withdrew financing for the film at a late stage, Harrison stepped forward and guaranteed the production with his own money for the charming reason that, as Cleese later explained, 'he wanted to see it'. Subsequently Harrison found himself on the set in Tunisia in the autumn of 1978 in this one small scene.

Stories about this production abound. John Cleese had originally expressed a desire to play the role of Brian, though he says he also wanted George Lazenby to do it, for the simple reason that they could use the tagline 'George Lazenby IS Jesus Christ'. But the role went to Graham Chapman. Since the production couldn't afford a proper doctor, Chapman, a trained medic, used to hold surgeries after shoots and, rather neatly, heal the sick.

So George Harrison got to see the film – and be in it too. Strangely, though, that isn't his voice. His one word uttered was lost in the

hubbub of the scene. It's simply 'ullo' in a thick Liverpool accent, addressed to Chapman, who isn't taking much notice of him. The speech was later dubbed and is, in fact, uttered by Michael Palin.

THE LORD OF THE RINGS: THE TWO TOWERS
2002
DIRECTED BY PETER JACKSON

At the time, Andy Serkis (the actor who portays the character Gollum in *Lord of the Rings*) thought he was going to New Zealand for three weeks of voice-over work on *The Two Towers*. But not long after his arrival he was on location, pioneering a completely new form of technology, in a freezing rock pool.

The scene where Gollum catches fish in the 'Forbidden Pool' is a great favourite for YouTube mash-ups – maybe it's his crooning little song, maybe it's the chomping on the raw fish. The Forbidden Pool, he sings, is 'nice and cool'.

Gollum, or Sméagol, is deformed by his long possession of the malign magical ring now in the hands of Frodo Baggins, played by Elijah Wood. He is playing along with Baggins for now, hoping to seize the ring back in an unguarded moment. He cuts a disgusting figure, with greyish, almost translucent skin, strands of hair drawn across his skull-like head, a sibilant way of talking and a reptilian way of moving.

The Gollum glimpsed in the original film is completely different from the one we see in *The Two Towers*; this Gollum was thrust into being when director Peter Jackson decided to use Serkis's own physicality to drive the character. Jackson's WETA digital company as good as went back to the drawing board, binning years of work, to get the results you see in this scene.

The main technique was motion-capture, for which Serkis donned a skin-tight suit covered in dots. Another innovative postproduction method included something called 'subsurface scattering', which allowed for the newt-like translucence of Gollum's flesh.

Gollum was ultimately modelled into a plasticine maquette or small-scale model. According to the 'creature supervisor' Eric Sainden, the maquette had 'three hundred muscles or more' and a full skeleton. Over 250 facial shapes were captured to manipulate his expressions.

Serkis modelled the Sméagol/Gollum voice on, he later said, the sound of a cat coughing up a hairball. Lacerating his vocal chords in the process, he was obliged to drink a special formulation laced with honey, just to keep his voice operational. Another source for the Gollum manner, according to Serkis, was the craving, wheedling manner of someone going through heroin withdrawal. His own family

members were also thrown into the mix – including his father and his two-year-old son.

Serkis did a fair amount of work in studio, but this trip to the rock pool was one of his relatively rare stints of onscreen, live acting. An early morning shoot revealed a ground covered in snow and ice; all of this had to be removed before filming started.

Serkis, wearing virtually nothing, dipped in and out of the pool as his character tries to catch a fish. Nice and cool? In fact it was freezing. And a long way from the nice warm studios where Serkis had expected to be doing his voice-over work.

THE MATRIX RELOADED
2003
DIRECTED BY ANDY AND LARRY WACHOWSKI

There's nothing like a good car chase. One of the most lavish was designed by the Wachowski brothers for their sequel to *The Matrix*. Filming their two follow-ups back-to-back, it was *The Matrix Reloaded*, rather than the final damp squib *Matrix Revolutions*, that contained their no-holds-barred, burning-rubber, fender-bending state-of-the-art car chase. It's never really been equalled. It took 45 days to film for a breathless 14 minutes of onscreen time, and it made use of a massive San Francisco set that was later re-used in a most unexpected manner.

Initially, a stretch of road (Route 59) in Akron, Ohio, was considered for the scene, but the practical problems of using a real road posed almost insurmountable challenges. Instead the Wachowskis built, from scratch, and at a cost of $2.5 million, a fake freeway on a disused naval base at Alameda in California which had been decommissioned in 1997. The entire mile-and-a-half road was fenced with a 19ft wall actually made from timber and plywood; the two overpasses were made to look like concrete.

The sequence is spectacular. There are new and old villains pursuing our heroes, wraith-like dreadlocked entities wielding cut-throat razors and guns, robotic secret-service types spraying the speeding Cadillac with bullets as it weaves to avoid them, Carrie-Anne Moss delivering motorcycle accelerations way beyond human ken and physical ability, cars rolling and cartwheeling into terrifying crashes, and good old Laurence Fishburne deploying some slick Taekwondo moves and samurai sword balletics on top of a speeding rig.

The sequence is especially beloved by *Matrix* nerds keen on the arcane significance of various road signs and truck signs you see along the way, including logos referring to *Gulliver's Travels*, the oft-repeating numeral 101 and an exit signboard to Paterson Pass which is allegedly a reference to the production designer, Owen Paterson.

General Motors donated well over a hundred cars for the scene, all of which were trashed. Intriguingly, many of the moments which look like CGI are not: when Agent Johnson spectacularly jumps on the bonnet of a speeding car and crushes it, it is in fact a real-time stunt with the car designed to buckle and roll.

Many people could film an entire movie in 45 days with $2.5m, but the Wachowski brothers wanted to pull off a spectacular. *Matrix Reloaded* eventually proved the greatest financial success of the trilogy.

And the fabricated freeway? Its 10,000 tons of timber were carefully dismantled and sent to Mexico, where the wood was used for the construction of a hundred low-income homes by a charitable organisation called The Reuse People. All that fictional mayhem proved one of the most socially responsible pieces of filmmaking in recent years.

METROPOLIS
1927
DIRECTED BY FRITZ LANG

In a dazzling special effect, an eerie robot woman is brought to life by a dastardly scientist. She will impersonate a revolutionary leader and become her evil twin. The automaton was played by German actress Brigitte Helm, then aged only 17; the director was Fritz Lang, whose torture of the actress is the stuff of legend. In a rather strange footnote, a then-unknown future actress-torturer assistant director happened to visit the Babelsberg film set in Berlin. Step forward Alfred Hitchcock.

Metropolis remains one of the most expensive movies ever made. Coming in at about $200 million in modern adjusted prices, it effectively ruined the studios who financed it. It also remains possibly the single most influential film ever made, with dreamlike and futuristic imagery that has permeated every nook and cranny of modern pop culture. It was the first film nominated for the UNESCO World Memory register in 2001 after its most recent reconstruction. Commercial cuts had acted on *Metropolis* 'as winds, rain, barbarians, etc. do upon classical edifice' in the words of filmmaker Stan Brakhage.

Shooting started on May 25th 1925 and lasted for over 310 days. Apart from the eight main actors, Lang also employed 26,000 male extras and 11,000 female ones. There were 750 children, '100 negroes and 25 Chinese' on hand as well. The film tells the story of two cultures – a worker culture and their sybaritic upper-class overlords. When a woman named Maria starts to rally the workers in a kind of Marxist rebellion, a scientist named Rotwang is commissioned to develop an automaton to impersonate her and ruin her standing.

The creation of this automaton (the Czech word 'robot' was not commonly used at the time) is the key scene of the movie – out of rings of concentric light she comes alive in the laboratory and the face of Maria is melded to her own. Filming took weeks of trial and error and involved a kind of 'liquid wood' being moulded to Brigitte Helm's body. The adolescent Helm was still growing and the armour required constant adjustment. Because it was moulded to fit her standing, a last-minute decision by Lang to film her seated caused the actress excruciating pain. The special effects were masterminded by camera-

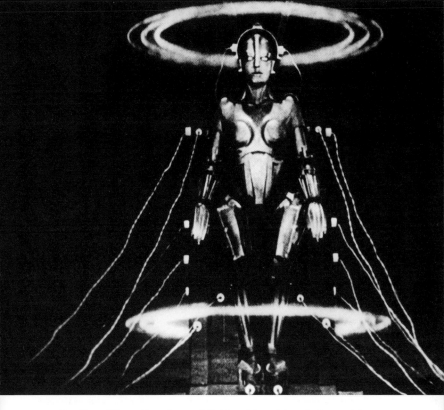

man Gunther Rittau, the rings of light achieved by photographing a small silver ball whirling against a backdrop of black velvet.

It was not over for Helm, and in a later scene in the film her costume caught fire. By 1935 she had retired from the movies altogether, and became a recluse in Switzerland where she died in 1996. At the time, when Hitchcock visited the enormous futuristic set and observed Lang at work, he was only months away from his own directorial debut. Both directors later claimed to despise each other's work.

THE MISSION
1986
DIRECTED BY ROLAND JOFFE

The Iguazú Falls is the startling natural phenomenon that opens *The Mission*, as a Jesuit priest, insensate and tied to a giant wooden cross, is hurled 80 metres downwards to 'The Devil's Throat' and the Parana River.

This waterfall appears in two other important scenes. One is where Robert De Niro is reduced to tears after climbing up its damp and rocky outcrop – a penance for his slaver crimes. The other is in the closing minutes. It's a long and gruelling scene, and in the days after it was filmed, associate producer Iain Smith recalls, the production had a visit from the Argentinian authorities over claims that a real massacre had taken place.

It took four villages and a 3,500-mile journey to re-create the lost world of the Guarani, a Paraguayan indigenous people whose exter-mination at the hands of Portuguese armed forces in the 1750s forms the climax of *The Mission*. Initially director Roland Joffe had intended to use the real tribe, but after discovering that the Guarani people had been decimated over the years, he looked elsewhere.

He found suitable candidates in the Waunana tribe of Colombia, a tribe that has since been decimated by FARC guerrillas and a spill-over of cocaine cultivation since 1986. These near Stone-Age people had barely seen a white man at the time *The Mission* came to call, much less watched a movie. They were puzzled by what making a movie might entail. In an eerie echo of the themes of the film, some even believed that they might be tricked, killed and possibly eaten by the British production team. But in the end the filming was arranged amicably, and the production donated agricultural goods and educational materials to the value of $90,000 to the villagers.

Though a new village was actually built for them by Iain Smith, this was not used in the film. Joffe never filmed near their home in Colombia, instead favouring areas in the Santa Marta region in North Colombia where *The Mission* set was built. It was a huge logistical operation: 350 people, including three babies born during the production, had to be moved to where the filming took place. The river scenes are cross-cut from separate locations, but the sharp-eyed can see the different vegetations of the two zones.

At one point two canoes, bristling with people, are flung over the edge of the falls into the abyss. These are articulated dummies being used here, apart from one shot, where a live actor makes a short jump. The shot was filmed several times, and as it happens many dummies were used. Many floated away, emerging five miles further south.

Shortly afterwards local papers started to report evidence of bodies glimpsed in the toiling waters, and dark rumours emerged of a terrible secret massacre upstream.

Iain Smith was a little red-faced when an army chief came to call, and the truth about the 'bodies' emerged. 'They laughed,' says Smith. 'They took it all in excellent good humour.'

OLDBOY
2005
DIRECTED BY PARK CHAN-WOOK

> "THE PROPS DEPARTMENT HAD ORDERED A TOTAL OF SEVEN OCTOPI FROM THE FISH MARKET. IT WAS ONLY ON THE SEVENTH TAKE THAT THEY GOT THE FINAL SHOT ... BEFORE EVERY TAKE WE HAD TO DO A PRAYER TO APOLOGISE TO THE OCTOPUS FOR KILLING IT. ... IT TOOK [CHOI MIN-SIK] A LONG TIME TO RECOVER."
>
> PARK CHAN-WOOK

The shot of South Korean actor Choi Min-sik chowing down a live octopus in *Oldboy* 'has become an iconic image in the minds of many Asian cinema fans,' according to film industry bible, *Variety*. It's one of the very few shots that didn't feature in the original Japanese Manga on which the film is based. The actor had to go to extraordinary lengths in the search for the perfect take, as director Park Chan-wook was to tell me.

The scene goes as follows. Choi's character has fought his way out of an inexplicable incarceration after 15 gruelling years of mind games and private torment. He has been held there for reasons which are, for the time being, mysterious. He is now at large in the city, in front of a sushi bar where he receives a wallet of money and a mobile phone from a passer-by. He enters the bar, and sits on one of the red-upholstered bar-stools.

'I want to eat something alive,' he intones dully to the pretty woman serving as a sushi chef. He's given a whole octopus on a green plate. The phone rings, and it's a phone call from his tormenter. After hanging up he rips off the head of the octopus and chews on the tentacles, which sucker and writhe around his face and even creep

into his nostrils. He faints face-down onto the sushi counter as the tentacles still wriggle from his lips.

'I want to say straightaway that most people in Korea don't normally eat octopus of that size,' reveals Chan-wook. 'But it's true we do eat it when it's still alive.' Park wanted to show the 'hatred' Choi's character felt after that mocking phone-call from his invisible tormentor, but also his desire to 'touch' after not being in contact with a living thing for 15 years.

'We filmed past midnight in a real Pusan restaurant called Gozen,' says Park. 'The props department had ordered a total of seven octopi from the fish market. It was only on the seventh take that they got the final shot they wanted with the tentacles really moving around in a good way.'

It turns out that each time was torture for Choi Min-sik, who, despite his formidable action presence, is a committed Buddhist. 'Before every take we had to do a prayer to apologise to the octopus for killing it,' recalls Park of that evening.

'It was very hard for him to kill something like that, let alone seven creatures in a row. It took him a long time to recover.'

ON THE WATERFRONT
1954
DIRECTED BY ELIA KAZAN

The scene is set in a New York taxicab and sits towards the end of Elia Kazan's *On the Waterfront*. It's usually held up – with some good reason – as the pinnacle of Marlon Brando's acting career, and depicts the moment where his character finally realises he has to stand up to the mobsters running the New York docklands: 'I coulda been a contender,' he says to his brother, played by Rod Steiger.

But not everyone appreciated Elia Kazan's parable of his anti-Communist stance, made just two years after he testified against his fellow artists in the infamous McCarthyite hearings. His representations to the 'House of Un-American Activities Committee' or HUAC blighted the career of many.

Elia Kazan was an ethnic Greek who was born in Istanbul and whose family emigrated to the US when he was four years old. In 1934 he joined the Communist Party but his stay in the Communist ranks was not a long one; after he became a successful Hollywood director he turned against everything they stood for. In 1952 he appeared before HUAC and supplied the names of eight people who had been fellow members of the New York Theatre group and fellow Communists in the 1930s. As a result of these eight names, the blacklist expanded exponentially. At the time he took out an advertisement in the *New York Times* defending his actions. 'I believe that Communist activities confront the people of this country,' he explained.

Two years later came *On The Waterfront* with Marlon Brando (Frank Sinatra was on standby for the role; Brando had a problem with those HUAC hearings until Kazan cunningly enticed him on board by playing him a screen test with his bitter rival Paul Newman). He plays the anguished young dockworker who decides to co-operate with the authorities at great personal risk to bring down the power of the ruthless gangsters then running the New York docks (the film was based on the Pulitzer prize-winning series of articles written by Malcolm Johnson in 1949).

Marlon Brando – who largely picked up his method acting style thanks to the encouragement of Kazan – later claimed in his autobiography that he had improvised the famous lines in the taxicab. But after an initial attempt at improvisation between the two actors,

Kazan told them to stick to the Budd Schulberg script (Arthur Miller turned down the opportunity to write it and to adapt his screenplay *The Hook*, since he too objected to Kazan's politics). Many of the solo shots of Rod Steiger were filmed after Brando had left the set for the day.

Rather ironically, one of the HUAC victims, Jules Dassin, ended up in Kazan's ancestral country of Greece – and lived till his death on a street named after his late wife, the actress and subsequently Greek culture minister Melina Mercouri. When Kazan tried to film his own novel *Beyond the Aegean* in Greece, Mercouri refused his request for the Greek army to be involved. Forty years after Kazan fed Dassin to the McCarthy wolves, Dassin's wife stopped his swan-song dead in its tracks.

ONCE UPON A TIME IN THE WEST
1968
DIRECTED BY SERGIO LEONE

The arrival of Henry Fonda as the bad guy in the second scene of *Once Upon a Time in the West*, where, smiling, he kills a defenceless small boy, sent shock waves through the American filmgoing public. For a decade, whenever the scene was shown on US television it was cut short, and the actual shooting was not depicted. Here was the man who had always been heroic – as Wyatt Earp and more significantly Abraham Lincoln, whom Fonda described as akin to playing Jesus Christ. But when he turned up in Europe just prior to filming, Leone was horrified by what he had done to his face.

By 1967 director Sergio Leone had made quite a name for himself as a director of spaghetti westerns, and he developed an early storyline for *Once Upon a Time in the West* after a chance meeting with Bernado Bertolucci in a cinema in Rome. Holed up with Bertolucci and Dario Argento, Leone worked out a plot which would take the idea of John Ford's *The Iron Horse* – one of the seven basic western storylines – a step further.

The scene was shot in Tabernas in Spain and was the first in which Leone and Fonda really clicked. A father is out shooting sand grouse with his son (the boy Timmy pretending to shoot apparently mimics Leone's fondness for child-like gunfights while discussing the movie). They return to their family home (incidentally made from lumber left over from Orson Welles's *Chimes at Midnight*) where a daughter is setting out a wedding feast and an older, teenaged son is late picking up his father's new bride from the train station. These are the McBain family – a name apparently chosen by the scriptwriters to honour crime writer Ed McBain – and a crooked railroad company wants their land.

After his bearded henchmen (wearing long coats called 'dusters', Leone being more authentic here than many a Hollywood western) have dispatched most of the family, Fonda strides into view, his baby blues flashing as he decides to shoot nine-year-old Timmy, rushing from inside the house with a bottle – like an altar boy late with the communion wine. Ennio Morricone's 'Like a Judgement' theme wells on the soundtrack.

If Fonda had had his way, his character would have looked very different. Just prior to filming he was sporting a moustache modelled on the assassin of Abraham Lincoln and wearing brown contact lenses to hide his famous eyes. 'Shave,' roared Leone when he first saw him in Rome, as recounted in Fonda's autobiography *My Life*. 'Where are the big blues? *That's what I bought!*'

He hadn't understood that Leone had wanted him to look like all the good guys he had ever played.

PERFORMANCE
1970
DIRECTED BY DONALD CAMMELL AND NICOLAS ROEG

> *"WHEN I LITERALLY CAME UP TO RELOAD THE CAMERA, NIC [ROEG] SAID S*D THIS, YOU'RE HAVING ALL THE FUN, AND DIVED UNDER THE BEDCLOTHES HIMSELF."*
>
> *MIKE MOLLOY*

By 1968 cinematographer Nicolas Roeg, who had distinguished himself with his work for François Truffaut (*Fahrenheit 451*) and John Schlesinger (*Far from the Madding Crowd*), had become a familiar figure in the demi-monde of Swinging London. In the summer of that year he put his contacts to good use by making *Performance* with Donald Cammell, a painter who had recently reinvented himself as a scriptwriter. They moved into a house in Notting Hill (25 Powis Square) and made one of the most groundbreaking films in British cinema.

The story is of a gangland boss who improbably goes to ground in the crumbling house of a rockstar minstrel played by Mick Jagger. There are two famous scenes involving the Rolling Stones frontman: one is the surreal 'Memo from Turner' sequence, a trippy fantasy in which Jagger dons a dapper suit and tie and starts behaving like a gangland boss. But the scene that caused the most aggravation was that of Jagger in bed with Anita Pallenberg and Michèle Breton. Mia Farrow was supposed to be the Breton character, but had broken her ankle.

A couple of large and powerful lights were aimed at the bed. Using a 16mm Bolex, camera operator Mike Molloy found himself under the sheets in what turned out to be a very long and very genuine sexual encounter between the three stars. 'When I literally came up to reload the camera, Nic said s*d this, you're having all the fun and dived under the bedclothes himself,' he later told Quentin Falk, who recounts the story in *Cinema's Strangest Moments*.

When the ten rolls of film were sent to the lab for development, Roeg found himself in trouble. The thousand feet of footage were

dubbed pornographic and consequently the lab risked prosecution for developing it. Roeg's employee Chris O'Dell was obliged to visit the premises and supervise the actual destruction of much of the material – using a hammer and chisel.

But some of the footage escaped the net, and according to one apocryphal source, was distributed in Holland as a porn film. The final bowdlerised version of the film (which still has four edits circulating – the cuts were ordered by Warners) was mostly finessed by Cammell after Roeg decamped to Australia to make *Walkabout*.

It remains something of an irony that Jagger's best and most memorable film role should actually be modelled on his friend and nemesis Brian Jones. Many years after the film's release, Jagger told author Colin McCabe that the myths still swirling around the film were 'so good I can't possibly deny them'.

Its themes still enthral British filmmakers, mostly drawn to its flavour of Kray-like gangsterism, urban decay and decadent rock stars. Guy Ritchie later bought the house in Queens Gate Mews where one of the scenes was filmed, and it was also featured in *Layer Cake*.

POLTERGEIST
1982
DIRECTED BY TOOBE HOOPER

The final and cataclysmic destruction of the haunted house in *Poltergeist* was one of the last great model-inspired special effects before CGI became the norm. It cost well over $25,000 to make.

Directed by Toobe Hooper and produced by Stephen Spielberg at the same time he was directing *ET*, *Poltergeist* is the story of an ordinary suburban family who buy a new house only to discover that they share it with a number of supernatural entities. In several famous scenes Steven Spielberg rehearses his own childhood fears – a devilish tree outside a bedroom window and a clown puppet with a talent for strangulation. Some of the scenes have their haunting quality precisely because they are filmed in one take: the chairs piled up on each other in the kitchen really were put together very quickly by props technicians in real time before the camera swings back.

The house used in *Poltergeist* still stands in Simi valley, and Spielberg sent over his Industrial Light and Magic wizards to measure every inch of it for a detailed reconstruction. Even the furniture was re-created in miniature. Measuring about six feet wide, the model was built with a hundred concealed wires. Chief technician Richard Edlund and machinist Gene Whitman then placed the house over a powerful vacuum machine and the camera was locked in place above it all. At the signal, the wires would be pulled, the house would collapse, and all the debris would be sucked inside.

This black-hole effect, where all the debris vanishes into a single point, is the key aspect to this special effect. Filmed at 300 frames a second, the effect was slowed down more than 15 times for the final version you see.

Though the sequence was slightly under-exposed, Spielberg was happy with the result. He had personally discovered the blond-haired little girl who was to become the star of the film, Heather O'Rourke, at the caféteria at MGM. At the same time, it was Drew Barrymore's audition for *Poltergeist* that landed her the role in *ET*; Spielberg decided he needed someone a little more angelic for *Poltergeist*.

Heather's death only a few years later has contributed to the 'curse of *Poltergeist*' legend. She was 13 when she died of cardiopulmonary arrest; her mother later sued the hospital in question. Dominique

Dunne, who plays Heather's older sister Dana, was murdered by her boyfriend before *Poltergeist* was even released. Both stars of the film are buried in the same cemetery at Westwood Memorial Park.

After the model was destroyed, its fragments were gathered up and deposited in a Perspex cube. Spielberg has kept it ever since on a grand piano in his Amblin offices.

PRETTY WOMAN

1990

DIRECTED BY GARRY MARSHALL

Richard Gere, playing a lonely multi-millionaire, has a surprise for Hollywood hooker Julia Roberts.

She's just dolled herself up for a night out at the opera. She's wearing the most astonishing red velvet dress and long white gloves. Gere has one last romantic gesture planned before he whisks her off to his private jet and *La Traviata* in San Francisco. He produces a long jewellery box and inside it lies a sparkling $250,000 Fred Joailliers diamond necklace. Roberts hungrily leans over to pick it out. Just as she does so, Gere snaps the box shut on her fingers and Roberts lets out a nervous, infectious, trilling laugh. What had been cooked up as a blooper moment for the out-takes reel was deemed so delightful it stayed in the movie.

It's fascinating to think what might have been. There's a clue in the movie's initial title, *Three Thousand* – her character's weekly dollar rate for Gere. In the early script Roberts has a serious cocaine addiction, and the whole business ends with the Gere character kicking her out of his car with a final shot as she goes off to Disneyland with her hooker girlfriend. It was destined to be a dark Indie drama about the seamy side of life – yet it morphed into one of the most popular fairytales in Hollywood history.

Initially the producers too had resisted casting the (then) lesser-known Roberts (despite an Oscar nomination for *Steel Magnolias*). Disney wanted Meg Ryan for the role, and Molly Ringwald turned it down. And when they brought in director Garry Marshall, the die was cast – a man who had cut his teeth on *Happy Days* was bound to go for the lighter touch. He threw out all the feelbad scenes and introduced the Cinderella meets Pygmalion gloss as corporate raider Gere slowly falls for this feisty hooker while staying at the Regent Beverly Wilshire.

The film became one of the most profitable ever made. Roberts became a superstar overnight. Gere found his career briefly enhanced. Most think of the Rodeo Drive boutique show-down (revenge on an uppity saleswoman) as the most memorable scene. But that unself-conscious laugh on the outset of the 'opera dream date' sequence became something of a trademark for Roberts.

PSYCHO
1960
DIRECTED BY ALFRED HITCHCOCK

The 45 seconds of the Hitchcock-directed shower scene in *Psycho* changed cinema forever. In a terrifying sequence, actress Janet Leigh is stabbed to death by a deranged motel owner played by Anthony Perkins. But the shadowy assailant, briefly glimpsed, is not Anthony Perkins at all; he was three thousand miles away at the time, in New York, rehearsing for a new Broadway play called *Greenwillow*. And the hand holding the knife? It's Hitchcock's.

Based on a 1959 novel by Robert Bloch, *Psycho* tells the story of a Phoenix secretary Marion Crane (Leigh) who steals $40,000 in cash from her boss and then flees the town. Audiences weren't used to the main character being killed off halfway through a movie, but this is exactly what Hitchcock did. Booking into a lonely motel in a Californian backroad, Marion Crane has the unfortunate fate to be murdered by the motel owner Norman Bates (Perkins), dressed up in the clothes of his dead mother.

Hitchcock meticulously storyboarded the scene, which was shot last, and a whole host of myths have grown up around it. One is that Hitchcock forced his lead actress to shower in cold water, a myth still perpetrated by Universal Studios on their set tours for tourists, but which Janet Leigh always denied. Hitchcock himself was not above spreading rumours; in an interview with Truffaut he claimed that the knife is never shown actually entering the woman's flesh, but further study shows that in three frames, it actually does. However, the 'blood' shown gurgling down the drain really is chocolate sauce – Hitchcock was impressed with how it looked in black and white.

The entire sequence only lasts 20 seconds, but the use of music – those stabbing strings scored by Bernard Herrmann – was revolutionary at the time. Hitchcock, whose career was showing signs of waning in the late 1950s, and who had not been given a generous budget by the studios, had produced his biggest commercial hit. Janet Leigh was haunted by the scene till her dying day: she had spent a week in the shower, dressed in a body-stocking, for the 70 odd takes of three seconds each. She was unable ever to shower again. 'It's not a hype,' she told a biographer, 'not something I thought would be good for publicity; honest to gosh it's true.'

And the identity of the figure in a dress who attacks Marion Crane in the bathroom? The full-length shots were of 24-year-old stunt-woman Margo Epper. Unlike the left-handed Perkins, she is holding the knife in her right hand.

RAIDERS OF THE LOST ARK
1981
DIRECTED BY STEVEN SPIELBERG

After three months of filming in Tunisia, Steven Spielberg and the crew of *Raiders of the Lost Ark* were beginning to feel the heat. Spielberg was still licking his wounds from a rare box-office failure – the now largely forgotten *1941*, a dismal WWII comedy which had bombed the previous year. He's rumoured to have taken with him crates of comfort food to get him through the shoot – cans and cans of Spaghetti Hoops, to be exact. It was probably the reason he was the only person on set who didn't go down with a bad case of gippy tummy.

Raiders of the Lost Ark began as a holiday conversation between George Lucas and Steven Spielberg in 1977. On the beach in Hawaii the two reminisced about the TV and comic book adventures of their childhood. Lucas mentioned an idea for a similar-themed film he'd already talked about with director Philip Kaufman: what if the Biblical Ark of the Covenant fell into the hands of Hitler's agents shortly before the outbreak of the war?

By the time a working script had been hammered out, the character that was to be known as Indiana Jones – the grizzled, self-mocking archaeologist action hero – was key to the movie. Nick Nolte passed on the role and Tom Selleck too; Harrison Ford was eventually cast. He was perfect as Indiana, thoroughly old-school in every way, tetchy and macho. He may not actually have been a Robert Mitchum or a Humphrey Bogart, but at least he could suggest them.

In one of the best-known moments in the movie, an assassin dressed in black and with a red waistband confronts Indiana in a Souk in Cairo. Marion, played by Karen Allen, is about to be abducted after she unwisely hides in a convenient rattan basket. Indy hasn't much time. But the looming Arab swordsman has plenty – he loops his gleaming scimitar in skilful arcs of light. He is going to take a horrid delight in showing his skill, killing this Infidel American.

Indy, on the other hand, doesn't even bother to reach for his bullwhip, his usual weapon of choice. Without the merest hint of fair play he shoots the swordsman down with his pistol.

As it happens, the script had allowed for many minutes of choreographed fighting. But Harrison Ford had other things on his mind. He needed to use the bathroom. He had diarrhoea. He needed

to make it quick. This comically improvised scene proved such a hit with the director that he junked the written scene and left it in.

RAISE THE TITANIC!
1980
DIRECTED BY LEW GRADE

> *"IT WOULD HAVE BEEN CHEAPER ... TO LOWER*
> *THE ATLANTIC."*
>
> *LEW GRADE*

'It would have been cheaper,' Lew Grade said famously, chewing furiously on a cigar, 'to lower the Atlantic.'

The money-shot for *Raise the Titanic!* was obvious – the vessel itself finally emerging from its watery grave before, preposterously, the US navy tows it into port. The ship you see arriving in New York is in fact the Greek vessel Athinai; made before Robert Ballard discovered the actual Titanic on the seabed, it was assumed by the producers of the movie (and by Clive Cussler, who wrote the original novel) that the ship remained intact, two and a half miles below sea level.

The vessel that rises from the deep is in reality a model that cost £5 million to make – only £2 million less than the actual Titanic in 1912. At 55½ft long, the model had exactly the right number of portholes. After they had finished building it, Grade learnt that that the original plan, to create a special tank at CBS studios, would have to be abandoned after unforeseen problems emerged to do with the geology of the site. After a great deal of horse-trading, the Maltese government gave the film permission to build a 'deep water facility'.

It required nine million gallons of water to fill the facility; specialist pumps from Holland were needed to drain the water overnight. It took ten months to build and cost £3 million, a sum so large it was mentioned in Malta's national budget of 1979. The prow of the vessel – later such a famous part of the *Titanic* movie starring Leonardo DiCaprio – was controversially rearranged to resemble that of the Athinai.

Unbelievably, there was still no consensus on how the money-shot would actually be managed, right up to the moment it was filmed. The 17-ton-per-square-foot pressure on the underwater model produced unusual technical problems. At one point a special steel gantry was designed to raise the model, and built at a cost of $200,000; but when

THEY'VE FOUND THE TITANIC! THERE'S JUST ONE THING LEFT TO DO...

RAISE THE TITANIC

it arrived from the US it was found to be 40 feet too short. The problem was eventually solved by a relatively crude method, the model being strapped onto a dolly-style platform and literally dragged along rails to the surface with a cable hooked to a vehicle.

The movie opened and failed to make back even a fifth of its budget. The original model can still be seen in Kalkara, Malta, in a state of advanced deterioration. It was last used in 1991 for a six-hour mini-series about the Titanic's sister ship, HMS Britannic. Clive Cussler's two decades of anger at his book's treatment by movie-makers came to a head when he foolishly allowed the making of *Sahara* in 2005 – another of the worst movies ever made. Cussler subsequently launched a lawsuit against the producers.

RESERVOIR DOGS
1992
DIRECTED BY QUENTIN TARANTINO

It's the infamous ear-cutting scene in the warehouse. The soundtrack: *Stuck in the Middle with You* on K-Billy's 'Super Sounds of the 70s Marathon' playing on the car radio.

Mr Blonde – aka actor Michael Madsen – is in the process of torturing a young policeman called Marvin (Kirk Baltz) after the heist-gone-wrong story reaches its zenith. After tying him to a chair and interrogating him, he tapes the cop's mouth shut and drawls, 'It's amusing to me to torture a cop.'

He performs an intricate and psychotic dance to a song recorded from the radio, teasing a cut-throat razor across the man's face before sawing off his right ear. Then he wanders outside, gets a can of gasoline from the trunk, douses his captive with it and prepares to ignite the gasoline with his cigarette lighter before a revived Tim Roth shoots him dead.

The warehouse, a former mortuary still stacked with coffins even at the time of filming, was torn down some years ago. It was at Figueroa St and 59th Avenue in Highland Park. Madsen's character was conceived as a vehicle for Christopher Walken, but he turned it down; the role was read for by George Clooney and for a while Tarantino had thought of Tim Roth as perfect for the part. Baltz auditioned for the policeman role four times before he got it. The line in the scene, mentioning that he has a child at home, was improvised by him; new father Madsen was so disturbed by this, and by the thought of Baltz's orphaned child, that he was unable to finish the first take.

The most alarming 'what if' is to do with the music. That 1972 Joe Egan and Jerry Rafferty song, written about a despairing meeting with record company executives and now indelibly associated with the 'ear scene' in *Reservoir Dogs*, was nearly not used at all. The alternative was Sweet's *Ballroom Blitz*.

And the fear in Kirk Baltz's face? You've guessed it – real. He had every reason to be nervous of Madsen. Earlier they had been prepping for the scene and Baltz made the mistake of suggesting that Madsen drive around LA with himself trapped in the boot. After all, that was really what his character had to endure.

LIVE ENTERTAINMENT/THE KOBAL COLLECTION

Madsen duly obliged. He threw the car around the highway, executed terrifying high-speed u-turns, and even stopped off for a burger on his way to the location – leaving Baltz in the hot, airless and claustrophobic trunk as he took his time, lingering on his meal.

'He looked real pissed off', Madsen recalls when he finally let his fellow actor – bruised and covered in sweat – out of his confinement. 'When I told Quentin he laughed for a week.'

ROSEMARY'S BABY
1968
DIRECTED BY ROMAN POLANSKI

The identity of the Devil in *Rosemary's Baby* has preoccupied occult conspiracy theorists for years. Was it really Anton LaVey, flamboyant high-priest of the Church of Satan? Who was inside that creepy rubber suit?

Rosemary's Baby was the first American film by Roman Polanski. It was based on the novel by Ira Levin, published only months before the film was made. The story concerns a nice middle-class woman living in New York who begins to suspect that her husband, neighbours and even obstetrician are a coven of witches and that she is about to give birth to the anti-Christ. The film rights to the book were bought by veteran film producer William Castle. In his autobiography *The Kid Stays in the Picture*, Robert Evans recalls forbidding Castle to direct the film as well, and how Polanski's preferred choice of Robert Redford (as Rosemary's malignant husband) was abandoned thanks to his ongoing legal row with Paramount over who produced the picture. In the end Mia Farrow was cast in the lead and filmmaker John Cassavetes played her husband.

In a key scene, Farrow, drugged with chocolate mousse, finds herself with her neighbours in a black magic ritual. She is lying prone. The Devil appears. He rapes her. Polanski framed the whole episode as akin to a drugs trip with no clear indication that this happens anywhere else except in the brain of Rosemary herself.

Farrow was not in a good state of mind at the time. Her husband Frank Sinatra had given her an ultimatum to leave the film by November 14th to take part in his own movie, *The Detective*. When she defied him, divorce papers were served to her on-set by Sinatra's attorney Mickey Rudin at the Dakota Building where they were filming. It's the same Upper West Side building where John Lennon went to live. He was murdered outside.

According to his daughter Zeena, Anton LaVey had absolutely no connection with *Rosemary's Baby* and he certainly wasn't wearing the Devil suit in the rape scene. Mia Farrow's body-double later recalled a 'young, very slender professional dancer' wearing the suit. This man's name was Clay Tanner, a bit-part player who also appeared in *Hello Dolly!* and many episodes of *Bonanza*. He died in 2002 without

recording his impressions of his most famous role, and almost nothing is known about him.

The suit, however, had a life of its own – it was bought by a Kentucky production company and re-used in a low-budget horror film called *Asylum of Satan* in 1971.

Having heard about the LaVey legend surrounding the suit, it was examined by the technical adviser of the film, Michael Aquino, who pronounced that the six-foot 200lb LaVey would never have fitted into it. Self-publicising fantasist LaVey had cooked the whole lurid story up.

SCARFACE
1983
DIRECTED BY BRIAN DE PALMA

> *"SAY HELLO TO MY LIL' FREN'"*
>
> *TONY MONTANA (AL PACINO)*

UNIVERSAL/THE KOBAL COLLECTION

Cuban druglord Tony Montana is holed up in his Miami mansion as gangsters pour onto his property, aiming to take him out for good. Upstairs in his office, Montana (Al Pacino) raises himself from his state of paranoid stupefaction, face down in a mountain of cocaine, opens his gun closet and grabs an M16 assault rifle with its M203 grenade launcher. 'Say hello to my lil' fren,' he roars, spittle-flecked, as he launches, single-handedly, into the invading goons.

It was Al Pacino himself who first came up with the idea of making *Scarface*. At the beginning it was intended to be a simple remake of the 1932 classic directed by Howard Hawks and produced by Howard Hughes. Proving too expensive to make in Chicago, the location was switched to sunny Miami, although the house used in the great showdown is located on the other side of America. This was deemed safer, since many Cuban-Americans had taken exception to the storyline, well-publicised even during the filming.

El Fureidis, which was put on the market in 2007 for $29m, is a ten-acre estate in Monteceito, California. It's a well-known property: Charlie Chaplin married Oona there, and its previous inhabitants include the German writer Thomas Mann, author of *Death in Venice*.

When asked to explain the film's popularity amongst hip-hop movers and shakers (P Diddy says he's watched it 63 times), director Brian De Palma noted, 'The hip-hop community was seeing all around them what was happening in the film – that cocaine makes you feel powerful, and you surround yourself with entourages and palaces and outrageous clothes and women, and you lose all touch with reality, you become numb.' And its most avid fans weren't just found within the hip-hopcracy. Saddam Hussein used the name Montana Enterprises for the international corporation he set up to launder his money.

If you look closely at one of the outside shots of El Fureidis, as a

small army invades Montana's house, you'll see a single uncredited shot from Steven Spielberg, who had dropped by to watch the filming. As for Al Pacino's encounter with his 'lil' fren', the rifle became so overheated from the blizzard of blanks being fired, he burnt his hands on the barrel. Pacino was obliged to sit out the last few weeks of production with his hands swathed in bandages.

THE SEVENTH SEAL
1956
DIRECTED BY INGMAR BERMAN

Put all thoughts of Keanu Reeves playing *Twister* with The Grim Reaper from your head. There's another, much-parodied scene right at the end of *The Seventh Seal* which has etched itself onto the minds of all who see it: the *Totentatz*, or Dance of Death, where Death leads his victims across a hillside skyline, helplessly dancing on his elongated rope like so many twitching and demented marionettes.

The premise of the film is starkness itself. A knight returns from the Crusades only to find Sweden in a state of anarchy – blighted by disease and convulsed by witch hunts and religious mania. The Grim Reaper, as if sensing his weariness and incipient decay, confronts him. But the knight ambivalently delays the fatal moment by challenging white-faced Death to a lengthy game of chess. It's a scene gleefully aped in films like *Bill and Ted's Bogus Journey*.

Made in only 35 days, with a tiny crew and a modest budget, *The Seventh Seal* emerged from a short morality play Ingmar Bergman had written in the early 1950s. At the time the film went into production, the director was attached to the Malmo Municipal Theatre and would customarily use the same loyal troupe of actors and technicians as he went from winter stagework to summer filmmaking.

Bergman cast a young Max von Sydow, one of the few actors to have played Jesus (*The Greatest Story Ever Told*) and the Devil (*Needful Things*), in the role of the disillusioned Crusader (a tussle with faith that was in some ways to be reprised when he played the eponymous Exorcist). Bergman, the son of a Lutheran minister, has a keen interest in religious imagery, if not much time for the Church itself.

PA Lundgren's set-designs mirror the frescoes Bergman saw as a boy when visiting churches with his father. Bergman's father was a man much possessed by damnation and darkness: the strict upbringing he gave young Ingmar (recalled in several of his films) included the small boy being locked in the cupboard 'with things that will eat your toes'.

There are several notable scenes in *The Seventh Seal* (Woody Allen's date movie in *Annie Hall*), but the final Dance of Death remains one of the single most indelible and famous images in cinema. As it happens, the scene was unplanned and improvised. After a long day's

shoot most of the actors and crew had gone home from the set, when Bergman observed an extraordinarily shaped cloud come over the horizon – a looming, apocalyptic cloud, no less.

The camera was hastily set up and Bergman pressed some electricians and even a few passing tourists for the scene. Of course, when Monty Python revisited it in *The Meaning of Life* the middle-class victims of the Grim Reaper all follow him in their Volvos – but that's another story.

THE SEVEN-YEAR ITCH
1955
DIRECTED BY BILLY WILDER

It's the most famous location shoot in Manhattan history – and it didn't even end up in the movie. Marilyn Monroe, wearing *that* Bill Travilla dress (a billowy, white crepe halter-top and sunburst-pleated skirt) is standing at the junction of Lexington and 52nd Street with the wind from the subway blowing her skirt up through a grille in the pavement. 'It's so delicious!' she trills.

Filming originally took place on Wednesday September 15th 1954, at 1 a.m. Marilyn was being her usual self – late for shoots, causing the film to run over-budget and over-time. She was notoriously unable to remember her lines, and this particular evening in Manhattan was no exception. She needed no fewer than 15 takes to nail a simple scene which involved walking out of a theatre and strolling down the sidewalk. At a key moment Monroe was to step over a grille and the breeze of a passing subway train would waft the dress above her head. It's said that the crew operating the fan took money from members of the public to crouch, like them, beneath the grille. Marilyn, as if anticipating just how much would be on show that night, took the precaution of wearing two pairs of knickers.

Monroe's husband Joe DiMaggio, who was present on the set, was incandescent with rage at the whole scene.

Director Billy Wilder hadn't quite reckoned how drunk and disorderly the neighbourhood crowd would be, even mid-week. Hundreds of bystanders stopped to gawp, cat-call and shout comments all the way through the shoot. The noise was astounding. The shots were later used for the posters – but the authentic Manhattan footage is not in the film.

Wilder had to re-create it all over again on the other side of America, in the back-lot of 20th Century Fox. Marilyn goofed just as many lines, but at least it was in the can. In the original edit the scene actually continues past the point in the film, with Marilyn exclaiming to co-star Tom Ewell, 'Bet you wish you wore a skirt – I feel so sorry for you in those hot pants.' The line was cut by the censors.

It's said that Monroe's marriage to DiMaggio never recovered from the experiences of that night on Lexington, and the couple divorced shortly afterwards.

The dress? The original is now owned by the actress Debbie Reynolds, but such is the power of the image that a copy, made by Travilla from his original design, was auctioned in December 2004 and fetched £37,000.

THE SHINING
1980
DIRECTED BY STANLEY KUBRICK

Jack Nicholson axing down the door and shouting 'Here's Johnny!' was voted the number one scariest film moment in a 2003 UK poll. The line was ad-libbed and the terror and exhaustion you see on the face of Shelley Duvall is genuine.

Warner executive, John Calley, had liked the original Stephen King horror novel. Kubrick thought little of King as a prose stylist, but when sent a copy of the book by Calley he was intrigued by its genre inventiveness. Though King had actually written a script for *The Shining*, Kubrick refused to read it. King also opposed Jack Nicholson's casting, but Kubrick had been looking to find a role for him since 1969. In consequence of these slights, the author's dislike of the film has remained implacable.

The exterior of the Overlook Hotel was shot outside the Timberline Lodge, near Mount Hood National Forest in Oregon. Kubrick refused to travel from his UK home to make the movie, so the interiors were constructed at Elstree studios, using four of their nine stages. Elstree had to juggle its production with *Flash Gordon* and *The Empire Strikes Back*.

The most striking technical aspect of the film was the novel use of Steadicam, its inventor Garrett Brown filming the famous gliding shots. Kubrick's lighting obsession was just one of many pressures on his actors: the 500,000 watts of luminescence generated temperatures of 110 degrees. Kubrick would characteristically reshoot a scene as many as 80 times and rewrote the script almost every day.

Shelley Duvall – a Robert Altman discovery – was Kubrick's first and only choice for the character Wendy Torrance. Five-and-a half year-old Danny Lloyd was cast as her son after an exhaustive casting process lasting six months and conducted in the US by Kubrick's trusted disciple Leon Vitali. Kubrick sat at home in St Albans, watching the tapes that Vitali sent over. Danny, who according to Kubrick never knew he was in a horror movie, grew up to be a biology teacher.

Kubrick's frequent verbal assaults on Shelley Duvall are said to be responsible for her nervous, harried look. That poster image of Duvall's face and Nicholson's demonic grimace always evokes Nicholson's ad-libbed line, 'Here's Johnny!'

Where did it come from? It was a reference to the classic introduction used by Ed McMahon when he ushered Johnny Carson onto
the *Tonight Show*.

SINGIN' IN THE RAIN

1952

DIRECTED BY STANLEY DONEN AND GENE KELLY

It's the best-known of all the Gene Kelly numbers: he tap-dances his way through a catchy song, splashing in puddles, swinging from lamp-posts and wielding his umbrella to emphasise his nimble choreography. He had a fever of 103° at the time.

The song was taken from *The Hollywood Revue of 1929* and the scene was to have been a trio with his co-star Debbie Reynolds and Donald O'Connor (two actors he famously terrorised – at one point Debbie Reynolds was found weeping under a piano by Fred Astaire, who then offered to teach her how to dance). The original idea can still be seen in the opening credits of the film, but *Singin' in the Rain* was destined to become Gene Kelly's calling card.

The film was made at the studios at Culver City in western Los Angeles, and two permanent streets were plumbed up for this particular scene. A complex system of pipes was used to create the rainfall, and special puddles made to key in to Kelly's choreography. Milk was mixed with the water to make it more visible to the cameras, and tarpaulin was used to shade the streets.

From the word go the shoots were arduous and long – sometimes up to 19 hours a day – and shooting had to be arranged around the sudden water-shortages that arrived every day at 2 o'clock. The reason for the sudden afternoon droughts? 2 o'clock was when the local residents at nearby Beverly Hills turned on their lawn sprinklers.

Days of water-logged rehearsals took their toll on Kelly's health, and he developed a raging fever at the time the scene was shot. His fine grey suit had also shrunk badly from all the dousings, partly restricting his movements. All the same he succeeded in 'becoming a kid again' for the purposes of the dance – emphasised by the dis-approving looks of a roving policeman played by Robert Williams (an extra and bit-part player all his life) which finally stop his antics.

Those famous Gene Kelly taps you hear sploshing in the rain are not actually his at all. His two choreography assistants Carol Haney and Gwen Verdon (Broadway star of *Can-Can*) post-dubbed them by standing ankle-deep in drums partly filled with water. This over-dubbing was common practice at the time, and elsewhere in the film it is Kelly's heels you can hear when Debbie Reynolds is dancing.

It's said that Kelly was so enraged by the scene's subversion in Stanley Kubrick's *Clockwork Orange*, for an especially violent rape scene, he ostentatiously snubbed actor Malcolm McDowell at a Hollywood gathering. It had been McDowell's idea to use the song in the first place, and Kubrick had liked the idea.

SOLDIER BLUE
1970
DIRECTED BY RALPH NELSON

Bear with me on this. In 1965, computing pioneer Ted Nelson invented the term 'hypertext'. This universal term is currently defined as when objects can be 'creatively linked' to each other. Now isn't that strange? Some five years later his father was connecting and disconnecting objects of a far fleshier and more visceral nature. Ralph Nelson, the Emmy award-winning film director all but forgotten these days, was hard at work designing the climactic scene of his film *Soldier Blue*.

His re-creation of the infamous Sand Creek Massacre of 1864 was to highlight acts of such visceral savagery and barbarism that it verged on exploitation cinema. In the days before digital effects, Nelson Snr went to bizarre lengths to get the on-screen blood-letting and wholesale amputations he required.

The film is now seen as a revisionist western riding the wave of the anti-Vietnam protests and most particularly the fall-out of the My Lai massacre – the 1968 atrocity when US soldiers went berserk and butchered 500 Vietnamese villagers. Ralph Nelson and his producers Harold Loeb and Gabriel Katzka wanted to make a movie that shocked people to the core. Whether its close-ups of bullets ripping through flesh and breasts being hacked off by bayonets remains anything more than exploitation cinema is still a matter of debate; certainly no DVD of the uncut version has ever been released in the US and it remains an awkward moment in the history of Hollywood.

The Sand Creek Massacre took place in Eastern Colorado, but Ralph Nelson filmed it in the Mexican Sierras. Peter Strauss plays the US cavalry officer pursuing a personal vendetta against the Cheyenne Indians after he survives a savage attack on a payroll train. When he rides into the Cheyenne reservation of Sand Creek one late November morning, he ignores the fact that the US flag has been raised in supplication, and orders his men to attack. The figures are vague, but between 150 and 200 men, women and children were slaughtered, often with their genitalia cut out, as well as 15 US cavalrymen.

Nelson went to town on the gory effects and a lorry full of prosthetics was parked on-set during the Sand Creek shoot; it was full of heads, legs and arms – as well as rubber breasts primed with

blood-bags and actual hospital limbs designed for amputees. And who was to wear them? Why the busloads of amputees, including children, whom Nelson hired after a sweep of Mexico City. Legs and arms were attached to the truncated limb – and then hacked off by a crazed soldiers. It was crude, but the effect remains startling.

Steven Spielberg was to include a version of the same event in his production of the mini-series *Into the West*, and it's said that the Sand Creek scene in *Soldier Blue* was the inspiration for the opening scene of *Saving Private Ryan*.

SOME LIKE IT HOT
1959
DIRECTED BY BILLY WILDER

It's probably the funniest 'curtain' line in Hollywood history – yet it was only dreamed up the night before filming, while the writer and director struggled with the script.

Some Like It Hot takes place in the 1920s. Two musicians are on the run from the mob. Jerry (Jack Lemmon) and Joe (Tony Curtis) are unwitting witnesses to the St Valentine's Day Massacre; disguising themselves as women they join a female musical troupe in a Florida beach resort. Their ploy works well until Curtis starts falling for fellow band member Sugar (Marilyn Monroe), and millionaire Osgood Fielding III (Joe E Brown) likes the look of Lemmon in drag.

In the final scene Jack Lemmon jumps into Joe E Brown's speedboat as he heads out for his anchored yacht. Lemmon feels the need to come clean to this affable, nautically themed suitor. 'Osgood, I'm gonna level with you – we can't get married at all,' he blurts. Osgood says he doesn't care, the same reply he uses when Lemmon also confesses he's not a 'natural blonde' and that he smokes.

'I can never have children!' Lemmon cries. 'We can adopt some,' replies Osgood. At which point Lemmon whips off his wig and exclaims with theatrical despair, 'I'm a man.' 'Well,' says Osgood, 'nobody's perfect!'

Much of the film had to be shot while making allowances for Marilyn Monroe's erratic behaviour. The last scene was written the night before expressly so that it could still be shot whether Marilyn turned up on-set or not. She was pregnant at the time and about to miscarry; look closely at some of her scenes and you can see her reading her lines from crib sheets pinned out of sight on the props. Though Curtis later denied he ever said that kissing Monroe was like 'kissing Hitler', her increasingly neurotic presence was resented by the cast and crew alike.

Though both Diamond and director Billy Wilder, if you can believe it, credited each other with the 'Nobody's perfect!' line, perhaps it's best to let Wilder have the last word on the subject, recorded by screenwiter Cameron Crowe in his *Conversations with Wilder*.

At the beginning of their script session the night before the scene was filmed, Diamond came up with 'Nobody's perfect!' Wilder hummed

and hawed, and then took an executive decision. 'Let's send it down to the mimeograph department so that they have something, and then we are going to *really* sit down and make a *really* funny last line.'

THE SOUND OF MUSIC
1965
DIRECTED BY ROBERT WISE

The Untersberg Mountain is located about 300km from Salzburg. It was on this mountain that Robert Wise shot the opening scene of *The Sound of Music*, in reality the last scene to be finished before the cast and crew returned to America. In it Julie Andrews throws her arms wide and sings *The Hills are Alive With the Sound of Music*. It's a truly ecstatic moment, and one of the most giddy helicopter swoops in cinema history.

The Sound of Music was a Broadway musical in turn adapted from the book *The Von Trapp Family Singers* by Maria Von Trapp. It's the story of a nun who becomes a governess to a wealthy Austrian family on the eve of Hitler's rise to power. Many of the details were altered from the true story – the Von Trapp's eldest child was a boy, not a girl, and the repertoire of the Von Trapp family was entirely classical.

The Von Trapps spent several more years in Austria after they married, and in fact fled to Italy, not Switzerland, by train and not on foot. In order to make *The Sound of Music*, Fox had to buy up the rights for several German versions of the same story by Wolfgang Liebeneiner, made in the late 1950s.

Though in real life Maria Von Trapp was never a nun, or even a novice, and had been raised by socialist parents with almost no religious interests, in the Robert Wise film Maria is a scatterbrained nun without the necessary solemnity to take her calling seriously. Wise hired Julie Andrews on the strength of her performance in *Mary Poppins* (1964) and most of the film was made on location in Salzburg, which still makes good money from *The Sound of Music* tourist trade.

During the opening scene, Julie Andrews found it hard to stay upright in the downward blasts of the helicopter rotor blades. 'One of my most famous shots is the opening of *The Sound of Music*,' wrote Robert Wise, many years later. 'I was concerned that it might be too similar to the opening of *West Side Story*, you know, the aerial opening shot. But we couldn't come up with anything better so we went with it and it worked brilliantly. I told Julie [Andrews] that when the helicopter got too close to her to turn and that was the signal for it to back off. She did, and I matched the turn in a close-up, because I knew

you could cut on the action. It worked so well, that to this day many people remember it as being a single shot!'

There was one image he was keen not to get in the shot, however. Hitler's beloved summer retreat at Berchtesgarden – the infamous Eagle's Nest – can just about be seen from the summit of the mountain.

SPARTACUS: 'I'M SPARTACUS'
1960
DIRECTED BY STANLEY KUBRICK

In 2007, when it seemed like Prince Harry might be deployed with the British Army to Iraq, soldiers of his very own Blues and Royals regiment adopted a novelty T-shirt. It was a message to those enemy combatants hoping to target the third in line to the throne. 'I'm Harry,' they all trumpeted, echoing the 'I'm Spartacus' moment from the sword-and-sandals epic starring Kirk Douglas.

It's near the end of the film. Douglas is the defeated leader of a slave revolt brought to its knees by the combined might of several Roman armies. Demoralised, the remnants of his army sit on the stony ground as Crassus – played by Laurence Olivier – offers to spare their lives if they will only identify and surrender their leader. But when Spartacus stands and identifies himself, others also stand, claiming to be Spartacus – thus all dooming themselves to death by crucifixion (including unknown and uncredited actor George Kennedy, who went on to win an Oscar for *Cool Hand Luke* seven years later).

Despite the sombre nature of this scene of exalted heroism, it has since proved a lightning rod for parody and satire. Polio sufferer Ian Drury attracted some spluttering, misinformed criticism for writing his 1980 song *Spasticus (Autisticus)* in which all the band members claim to be 'spasticus'.

It's intriguing to think what the original screenwriter would have made of all this. Dalton Trumbo – damned by the McCarthyite House of Un-American Activities (HUAC) in the early 1950s – was struggling to overcome his studio blacklisting at the time when Kirk Douglas (also producing the film) decided to hire him and publicly break with the blacklist for the first time.

According to Vincent LoBrutto's biography of Kubrick, the director had at one point been happy to pass the screenplay off as his own; there was an outcry at Douglas's decision and various right-wing organisations threatened to picket the film. The scene of unity against an overwhelming force consequently had deep personal resonance for Trumbo, after the likes of Elia Kazan and Edward Dmytryk informed on their fellow writers and filmmakers to save their own skin.

More than 320 people 'with Communist affiliations' were placed on a list whose baleful influence lasted for a decade. They included

Orson Welles, Joseph Losey, Dorothy Parker, Leonard Bernstein, Charlie Chaplin, Arthur Miller and Dashiell Hammett. Nobody stood up and said 'I'm Spartacus' for them until Kirk Douglas came along with this movie (adapted from a book by the also-blacklisted Howard Fast) and, both figuratively and literally, stood up.

Ironically, much of *Spartacus* was filmed on land once owned by William Randolph Hearst, a keen supporter of McCarthy.

SPARTACUS: 'SNAILS AND OYSTERS'
1960
DIRECTED BY STANLEY KUBRICK

> *"THEY NEVER PLANNED TO PUT THAT SCENE IN*
> *THE MOVIE ... AND BOTH LARRY [LAWRENCE*
> *OLIVER] AND I OBJECTED. ... SO THEY DID IT IN*
> *ONE SHOT. NO COVERAGE. WE KNEW WE WERE*
> *IN TROUBLE RIGHT THERE."*
>
> *TONY CURTIS*

The re-issue of *Spartacus* in 1991 included a 'lost' scene. A previously unknown 'snails and oysters' moment with Laurence Olivier and Tony Curtis was discovered, without its original soundtrack, during a restoration project to re-integrate a lost 14 minutes of film from the Universal archives. Its omission has a curious history: it was dropped from the original 1960 edit after moral objections from both the MPAA and the Legion of Decency.

Spartacus was directed by Stanley Kubrick and starred Kirk Douglas as the hardened gladiator who leads a slave uprising in Rome in 70BC. As executive producer, Douglas had hand-picked 31-year-old Kubrick after a quarrel with Anthony Mann, also hiring blacklisted writer Dalton Trumbo for the script. An impressive cast included Charles Laughton as dyspeptic senator Gracchus, and Peter Ustinov Oscar-winning as sleazy slave-dealer Batiatus.

And what of the lost scene? Set in a lavish Roman marble bathroom at night, the slave Antoninus (Curtis) is having to attend to his half-naked master Crassus (Olivier). The air is heavy with possible gay seduction. 'Do you eat oysters,' purrs Crassus at the slave. Antoninus says that he does. 'Do you eat snails?' persists Crassus with a leer. 'No master,' gulps Antoninus. Crassus tetchily demands his robe. 'My taste includes ... both snails and oysters,' he says.

It isn't Olivier voicing the lines here; he had died many years earlier. Robert A Harris, the producer in charge of the restoration, had pulled in an aged Tony Curtis into an LA studio to read his old lines

from the original script (only Kirk Douglas had a copy). Approaching Olivier's widow Joan Plowright for suggestions, Plowright recommended one of Olivier's *protégés* from his early years at the National Theatre: Anthony Hopkins. Working from a fax sent over by Kubrick as to how the scene should be played, clever mimic Hopkins produced a wickedly accurate impersonation of his old mentor.

In 2002 Curtis recalled for *Metroweekly*, the Washington Gay and Lesbian online magazine, 'They never planned to put that scene in the movie – I remember when we were going to shoot it the studio said "maybe we won't". And both Larry and I objected. We said, "We want this scene in the movie." So they did it in one shot. No coverage. We knew we were in trouble right there.'

The 1991 version of the film, running at 187 minutes in the US, involved making a new negative and putting back several other short scenes, most of which had been omitted for their violence. But it's the salacious bisexuality of the 'snails and oysters' scene that struck a chord when it was included; it clarifies onscreen motives, such as why Curtis's character actually runs away from his master. The suggestion of the censors – that the offending snail and oyster words be replaced by 'artichokes' and 'truffles' – was, needless to say, never adopted.

STAIRCASE

1969

DIRECTED BY STANLEY DONEN

It's not often that visiting members of the British Royal Family disrupt the filming of a scene. But so it was with the little-known comedy from Stanley Donen (*Singin' in the Rain*) called *Staircase*, which features Rex Harrison and Richard Burton as hairdresser boyfriends living in Swinging London and boasts a musical score from Dudley Moore.

Rex Harrison, not an easy man to get along with, hated the film from the word go. He was mortally embarrassed to play a gay role and delivered a caricature of such viciousness that the film has rarely been screened since. Richard Burton, on the other hand – always rumoured to have been bisexual in the early days – regarded it as a perfectly amiable way of paying off those very high mini-bar costs.

The film was made in Paris, with the London flat built to order in a Parisian studio. At last the day arrived that Harrison had most been dreading; he had done everything in his power to get the thing deleted, but Donen had insisted that the scene was essential. He would be shown sharing a bed with Richard Burton.

Filming was scheduled for 4 p.m. Burton had been out lunching with Mrs Burton, Elizabeth Taylor, then also in France filming with Warren Beatty in *The Only Game in Town*, a drama set in Las Vegas. The production had actually been moved to France on Taylor's request. Naturally the couple invited along Burton's co-star, and other guests included Maria Callas and the Duke and Duchess of Windsor, who had lived in Paris almost full-time since the abdication.

One can only imagine Harrison sweating throughout the long afternoon and trying to be pleasant to the other guests. Then the scenario he was dreading came to pass. The Duke and Duchess of Windsor were invited on-set to watch the two stars filming.

Donen sensed the atmosphere and dispensed with the rehearsal, immediately ordering a take. By this time Burton, pleased to be in contact with a bed, immediately fell into a gentle slumber. Prodded into action, he awoke and promptly lost all recollection of where he was or what the lines were. The cameraman hissed some instructions – then lost his balance on the plank where he was perching and came crashing down between the two actors.

It was the perfect excuse for Harrison, purple with embarrassment and pique, to exit for his dressing room. After completing the film he didn't make another for four years, by which time his career was effectively over. Burton seemed unscathed by the experience; indeed, his scenes with his invalid mother, played by Cathleen Nesbitt, were deemed the best thing in this now-forgotten Odd Couple comedy-drama.

STAR WARS
1977
DIRECTED BY GEORGE LUCAS

How did a Warner Brothers stock sound effect become an in-joke amongst movie sound editors after being revived for the original *Star Wars* – and why is director Joe Dante now refusing to use it?

It's an insignificant moment in *Star Wars*. Luke Skywalker is on the Death Star, lair of his nemesis Darth Vader, and fighting a running battle with the white-armoured Storm Troopers. He's come to a vertiginous drop at the end of a corridor, but is taking the opportunity to fire upon the Storm Troopers in a similar position just opposite. One Trooper falls into the abyss between them and there's a strangulated, slightly high-pitched cry as he succumbs. This is the 'Wilhelm scream'. It has been used in more than 130 films since the 1950s, but this was the moment at which it became a cult item.

The man who put the scream into *Star Wars* is sound designer Ben Burtt. Burtt was looking through the Warners archives when he came across a 3D film called *Distant Drums* made in 1951. During a scene in which some soldiers are wading through the everglades, one is savaged by a waiting alligator. It's the first use of the Wilhelm scream. Why is it Wilhelm? Burtt dubbed it that after finding a subsequent use in *The Charge at Feather River* (1953) where it is issued by one Private Wilhelm (played by Ralph Brooke) after being shot in the leg.

For years the scream was only ever heard in Warner Bros films: it's on the soundtrack of Judy Garland's *A Star is Born*, amongst many others. After Burtt started using it as a *leitmotif* in all of his movies it became much better known.

During the editing of *Reservoir Dogs*, Quentin Tarantino called for a break when he was told the history of the scream just as he was using it; he immediately crowded into a nearby room with his sound crew so he could watch *Distant Drums* on a local TV station – it happened to be playing.

Joe Dante regularly employed the Wilhelm scream as a zombie cry in his films, although more recently he has abandoned its use. Now everyone is in on this former industry joke, a bit of sonic badinage between special effects experts.

Who screamed the Wilhelm scream? The most likely candidate is Sheb Wooley (famous for the song *The Purple People Eater*, which sold

3 million copies in 1958). Originally a bit-part actor, he played the uncredited role of Private Jessup in *Distant Drums* and was, it seems, hauled into Warners for some post-production screaming.

TAXI DRIVER
1976
DIRECTED BY MARTIN SCORSESE

> "YOU TALKIN' TO ME? YOU TALKIN' TO ME? YOU
> TALKIN' TO ME? THEN WHO THE HELL ELSE ARE
> YOU TALKIN' TO? YOU TALKIN' TO ME? WELL I'M
> THE ONLY ONE HERE. WHO DO YOU THINK
> YOU'RE TALKING TO? OH YEAH? HUH? OK."

Travis Bickle is practising with his guns in front of a mirror in one of the most-quoted scenes in modern cinema. The film is *Taxi Driver*; the actor is Robert De Niro. One of the last scenes to be shot, why was this famous dialogue improvised by De Niro?

The film's story is simple enough. It's a mood piece, a love-hate letter to New York in the era of 1970s urban decay and chequered cabs. De Niro plays the alienated Vietnam vet Travis Bickle, who drives a taxi for a living. Scriptwriter Paul Schrader based his character on the case of Arthur Bremer, who had tried to assassinate presidential candidate George Wallace. Martin Scorsese's follow-up film was to be *King of Comedy* – perhaps an exorcism of the information that John Hinckley had become obsessed with *Taxi Driver* prior to his assassination attempt on Ronald Regan (the film is about a stalker). Travis Bickle's name is an homage to Malcolm McDowell's character in *If....*, *O Lucky Man!*, and *Britannia Hospital*, variously a schoolboy, coffee salesman and reporter.

Paul Schrader, an ex-critic turned top-dollar screenwriter, was a *protégé* of Brian De Palma, for whom he had written the semi-autobiographical *Taxi Driver* (drawing on his LA experience of a nervous breakdown). With De Palma's blessing, Scorsese took over the script with De Niro in the lead. Despite De Niro's recent *The Godfather II* Oscar win, the Hollywood establishment made clear its antipathy for the film at an early stage – the budget was hard to raise at a paltry $1.3 million.

In this last scene, Travis Bickle is enraged by the spectacle of Jodie Foster as an underage child prostitute, and decides to arm himself with a small arsenal of handguns and ride to her rescue. In the famous mirror scene here he is, stripped to the waist, practising his moves. The mixture of jump-cuts, reverse angles and 180-degree swish pans makes it hard to differentiate the man from his mirror image.

And the reason Bickle keeps repeating the line 'Are you talkin' to me'? According to one critic, this was a borrowed line from a stand-up comic. But the real reason? If the camera had panned down you would have seen Scorsese himself lying on the floor, mere inches from the actor, wearing headphones, mouthing to De Niro 'say it again' out of earshot – worried that the street-noise from bustling New York was ruining the take.

THE TERMINATOR
1984
DIRECTED BY JAMES CAMERON

Famous movie lines are usually a hair's breadth away from staggering banality. In *The Terminator*, the original James Cameron sci-fi movie which made a star both out of him and his lead actor Arnold Schwarzenegger, the line 'I'll be back' is a case in point.

Cameron has always said that his original inspiration for *The Terminator* lay in a single image that arrived unbidden in his mind one day; a nightmarish vision of a super-heated metal skeleton walking from a blazing inferno. This scene comes late in the movie, and from this point the rest of the film is essentially backward-engineered.

Earlier on, Schwarzenegger, who plays a human-imitation cyborg sent back in time to locate and assassinate Linda Hamilton, has tracked Hamilton to a police station where she is being questioned. He approaches the desk sergeant, who barely looks up as the Terminator addresses him in a broad Austrian accent. In one great shot, the Terminator looks up, apparently scanning the police station ceiling and the structure of the protective booth in which the sergeant sits, leans forward with particular menace and intones 'I'll be back'. And back he surely comes.

There's a close-up of the sergeant's paperwork, before, initially noiselessly, the Terminator drives his jeep straight through the doors of the station. There follows general mayhem and a big shoot-out; the Terminator's robotic vision, with its computer feeds created by Stan Winston and Fantasy II Film Effects, assists him on his killing spree. The graphics are actually the assembly code for the Apple II operation system. Essentially the Terminator is a big Apple computer.

Lance Henriksen was originally Cameron's choice as the cyborg killing machine; Cameron wanted someone rather ordinary looking and nondescript (he was later to cast Henrikson as the helpful android in *Aliens*). But Schwarzenegger made the role his own. He was constantly reprising the line 'I'll be back' in future films. It became his trademark.

What was it in the original script? 'I'll come back.' That's it.

Not much of a difference perhaps. Slightly more polite. Slightly less menacing. And yet 'I'll be back' is freighted with a menace that would have been quite absent if the scripted version had been used. In

popularity it has even eclipsed the grandstanding scene that Cameron built the film around, when finally, stripped of his synthetic tissue and skin, the Terminator steps from an inferno with one of the last great hurrahs for stop-motion special effects.

James Cameron later revealed that police officers constantly tell him the 'I'll be back scene' is their favourite scene in all his movies, something that puzzles him, considering that virtually the entire station is mown down by the Terminator in his customary two-gun spraying pose.

None of the subsequently over-franchised films and TV shows has matched its clever, low-tech thrills.

TWILIGHT ZONE – THE MOVIE
1983
DIRECTED BY JOHN LANDIS

On the night of July 23rd 1982, John Landis was about to finish filming a scene from *The Twilight Zone* on location at Indian Dunes Park, about 40 miles north of Los Angeles.

It was a plum role for fading character-actor Vic Morrow, and something of a comeback after a long battle with the booze. Landis was one of the most successful directors of his generation, and this feature spin-off of the cult 1960s supernatural TV drama featured several different stories stitched together in *portmanteau* fashion by four different directors. In *The Twilight Zone*, nightmares take place in waking life, where natural law is suspended. In Landis's section, Morrow plays a racist bigot getting a taste of his own medicine; he finds himself pursued by the Nazis and then lynched by the Klu Klux Klan. But the Vietnam war offers him a chance of redemption.

On the south shore of the Santa Clara River – a shallow, slow-moving stream that irrigates orange and avocado groves a few miles to the west – a Vietnamese Village had been assembled out of bamboo poles, palm thatch and cardboard. Two young Asian-Americans had been hired – illegally as it later turned out, their parents paid $500 in cash – to play the Vietnamese children his bigoted character has to save from a US firebombing raid in an act of redemption.

The filming the previous night had gone well and Vic Morrow had kept the children amused by making faces at them. But this last shot was much more dangerous, with pilot Dorcey Wingo having to fly a helicopter perilously near the actors as explosions happen all around.

After several hours of preparation in the Californian darkness, at 2.20 a.m. Landis ordered action. Vic Morrow was to cradle the Vietnamese children in his arms and wade across the river shouting, 'I'll keep you safe, kids! I swear to God!' as the village exploded in the background. Landis, on a walkie-talkie, and on a bullhorn, shouted 'lower, lower' to the helicopter as it buzzed around the fleeing figures.

Against all safe procedure, a court later found, the helicopter flew too close to the ground and lost control. The helicopter's right skid slammed into one child, killing her immediately. At the same time the main rotor ripped off Morrow's head and also the head, shoulder and arm of the other seven-year old. Though Landis was later cleared of

culpability after a ten-month trial, the Directors Guild of America censured him for 'unprofessional conduct'.

It's not well known, but Vic Morrow was the estranged father of actress Jennifer Jason Leigh. He left her a mere $100 from his multi-million dollar estate. The parents of the illegally hired child actors received millions of dollars in compensation.

UN CHIEN ANDALOU
1928
DIRECTED BY LUIS BUŇUEL

The opening scene of the Luis Buñuel movie *Un Chien Andalou* – a prologue in which a woman's eye is slit open with a cut-throat razor – originated in a conversation between Buñuel and his friend Salvador Dali on the subject of dreams.

Buñuel had spent the early 1920s at the Residencia de Estudinates in Madrid, where he knew both the playwright Lorca and the artist Dali, with whom he shared many artistic and political ideas. While staying with Dali at his house, Buñuel told Dali about a dream in which a cloud had sliced a moon in half 'like a razor blade slicing through an eye'. Dali responded that he too had dreamed a curious dream in which ants crawled from a wound in the hand. 'And what if we started right there and made a film?' ventured Dali – so they did. Both images were to end up in their 17-minute collaboration *Un Chien Andalou*, a lodestone of early cinema startling in its surrealism.

The opening begins with projected words *'Il etait une fois'* (Once upon a time) and the image of an observed moon. The man who watches it from a balcony is Buñuel himself, and he is honing a razor blade to perfect sharpness. Standing with a cigarette dangling in the right-hand corner of his mouth, Buñuel is seen preparing to slice open the eye of a woman who sits motionless beside him, and whose face replaces that of the moon.

Prising open her left eye, Buñuel proceeds to draw the slick blade across the exposed eyeball (actually a calf's eyeball obtained from a butcher). The woman is the essence of dream-like passivity as the viscous fluid of the eye leaks across the steel.

Though the rest of this short début is full of arresting images – grand pianos stuffed with the putrefying remains of a donkey and so forth – nothing would quite equal the opening shock of that slit eyeball image. Many decades later Buñuel would lay down the soundtrack actually used in the original performances, and for the first time since the 1920s the unnerving tango music that accompanies the first scene was heard again.

Buñuel's was the first film that set out to alienate and discomfit its audience, a completely new concept at the time. It was a film, according to Jean Vigo, rather in the spirit of things, that demands 'we must see

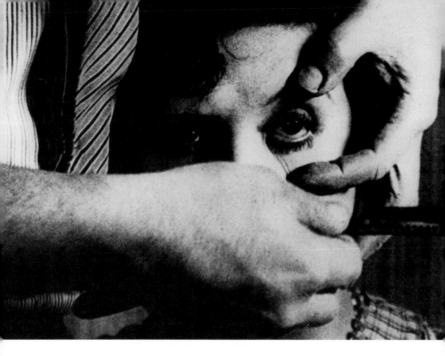

with a different eye'. Its lyrical, surrealist, anti-establishment qualities have been much borrowed by music video makers.

In the 1970s David Bowie even used the film as his 'opening act' during a concert tour. The whole work of David Lynch owes a particular debt to this one short film from Spain. 'Give me two hours of activity and I'll take the other 22 in dreams,' Buñuel later wrote.

VAMPIRE'S KISS
1989
DIRECTED BY ROBERT BIERMAN

> *"IN THE SCRIPT IT HAD BEEN WRITTEN THAT HE SHOULD EAT A RAW EGG ... I DISCUSSED IT WITH NIC [CAGE] AND HE SAID 'I REALLY WANT TO DO MY ROOM 101', WHICH HAPPENED TO BE COCKROACHES."*
>
> *ROBERT BIERMAN*

What's the true story behind the early Nic Cage film where he actually eats a live cockroach? And which famous movie director/comedian refused to believe that the scene was real?

These days, independent filmmaker Robert Bierman is better known for his work on UK television – most recently at the helm of *Waking the Dead*. But back in 1989 he was in New York making a feature film about a publishing executive who believes he's turning into a vampire. In this particular scene, Cage, increasingly demented, sees a cockroach on the hob of his kitchen cooker, pops it in his mouth, antennae wriggling, and crunches it up.

'In the script it had been written that he should eat a raw egg,' Bierman recalls. 'But a day or so before filming I'd seen a Japanese film *Tampopo* do the same thing. So I discussed it with Nic, and he said "I really want to do my room 101", which happened to be cockroaches.'

Filming in an apartment block opposite the Gramercy Park Hotel, the props manager went down to the basement and came back with a number of bugs. 'We had a bug beauty competition,' says Bierman. 'And we selected two.' There were two takes. 'He ate it, chewed it, and after the shot spat what was left out and took a shot of 100 per cent vodka.' Bierman asked him to do it again. 'In fact the second take wasn't so good, and the cockroach didn't move enough, so Nic flicked it with his finger to try and get some life into it.'

Cage later told a journalist, 'I couldn't really taste it, but psychologically it was murder – I couldn't eat anything for three days. I had

difficulty sleeping. Every muscle in my body didn't want to do it, but I did it anyway.'

In those days, a year before making *Wild at Heart*, Cage was fearless in his commitment to acting. 'He also ate a pigeon later on,' says Bierman. 'I had to drug them so he could catch them. Filming in the late 80s, there really were no health and safety issues. There was another scene where a bat flies around the room, and Nic had to be stopped from sending his assistant off to Central Park and catching a real one.'

Bierman was careful to shoot the scene in one unbroken shot to make it clear that no trickery was involved. Even so, he later received a phone call from filmmaker Mel Brooks, asking him for the address of his 'brilliant' props man who had so expertly faked the scene. Bierman had to assure him that Cage had, in fact, eaten a real, live bug from the basement.

WHATEVER HAPPENED TO BABY JANE?
1962
DIRECTED BY ROBERT ALDRICH

Marooned in her wheelchair, Joan Crawford is at the top of the staircase of the decaying Hollywood mansion she shares with her sister, played by Bette Davis. Painfully, slowly, she begins to drag herself down the stairs, clinging to the ornate metal balustrade, determined to reach the hallway where she can call for help. She reaches the phone after great effort, and calls her doctor, begging him to come round, claiming that her sister is violent towards her.

Just that moment, Bette Davis returns from her chores in West Hollywood with an armful of dry cleaning. There follows a vivid attack in which Bette Davis repeatedly kicks Crawford to the floor.

The scene is infamous in the long history of Hollywood feuds, since Davis really did kick Crawford in the head, quite badly too. Crawford was seriously bruised, and the gash on her head required three stitches. She was to get her revenge, later in the movie.

There are all manner of claims and counter-claims about the feud between these two queens of Hollywood. Crawford was every inch the glamorous film star and Davis made no bones about whom she thought was a proper actress; her theatrical experience and impressive string of Oscar nominations and wins gave her the edge, she felt. Each was jealous of the other and there was almost certainly an element of sexual rivalry between the two.

Davis had fallen in love with actor Franchot Tone when they acted together in the movie *Dangerous* in 1935 (the same year in which he received an Oscar nomination for his turn in *Mutiny on the Bounty*). During the filming at Warners, Tone would come back from encounters with Crawford covered in lipstick. Their engagement was announced before the shoot had ended, and Davis was left seething with jealousy.

Some have claimed that the feud was manufactured to promote the movie, and sometimes both actresses liked to claim it was all in the imagination of the gossips. But their quotes about each other are amongst the bitchiest in Hollywood. 'Miss Davis was always partial to covering up her face in motion pictures,' said Joan in 1973. 'She called it "Art". Others might call it camouflage – a cover-up for the absence of any real beauty.' On hearing of Crawford's death, Davis quipped, 'Just because a person's dead it doesn't mean they've changed.'

The stories are legion about the production; Davis had a Coca-Cola machine installed because Crawford was on the board of Pepsi. Crawford's bottles of Pepsi were half-filled with vodka. But most seem agreed on how Crawford got her revenge for the kicking. Later there's a scene where Davis has to drag Crawford from her bed. Crawford wore a belt full of lead weights under her costume, and Davis was lucky to get away without a serious injury to her back.

WHEN HARRY MET SALLY
1989
DIRECTED BY ROB REINER

Some restaurants have fared well from associations with famous movie scenes, but none more so than Katz's famous Jewish Deli at 205 East Houston St on the Lower East Side of New York City. It's where Meg Ryan conducted her much celebrated 'fake orgasm' scene in front of a bemused Billy Crystal.

Katz's Deli was founded in 1888 and found a ready consumer base for Russian immigrants; its moniker 'send a salami to your boy in the army' became famous in WWII. Now you can sit under a round sign hanging from the ceiling which reads (using the same signage and graphics, which may or may not be significant) 'Where Harry Met Sally – Hope You Have What She Had – Enjoy!'.

When Harry Met Sally has all the elements of classic Jewish comedy, and it's not remotely surprising that Meg Ryan and Billy Crystal end up in a temple of Jewish cuisine for this crucial scene. Director Rob Reiner developed the script with *Sleepless in Seattle* writer Norah Ephron, and he has always maintained that it comes from his own experiences of dating and divorce.

Both the characters Harry and Sally (Ephron always said she hated the title) are platonic pals who first meet at Columbia University and then happen to catch up again on several occasions over a ten-year period. Almost the entire movie revolves around an extended dialogue between the two, exploring the notion that men and women can't actually remain friends as sexuality will always get in the way.

During the Katz Deli scene Meg Ryan is also determined to prove to Billy Crystal that women are adept at faking orgasms, and proceeds, fully clothed and still at the dining table, to give a long and elaborate rendition of her theory.

By all accounts Meg Ryan managed to reshoot the scene for many hours as director Rob Reiner meticulously pushed for the perfect take. The original script had not actually included this theatre of engorgement – it was to be discussion only, with no practical demonstrations. Meg Ryan herself pushed for the idea, and Reiner liked it so much he wrote it into subsequent drafts.

Most people remember not just the Meg Ryan theatrics but also the funny line that ends them – offstage as it were. Just who is that

demure middle-aged woman with the greying hair and the somewhat unsightly brown woollen top who tells the waiter, 'I'll have what she's having!' when Meg Ryan finishes her howling, thereby virtually silencing the entire restaurant. Step forward Estelle Reiner – the entirely respectable mother of the director.

THE WICKER MAN
1973
DIRECTED BY ROBIN HARDY

In the fateful last scene of the cult British film *The Wicker Man*, Sgt Neil Howie – played by Edward Woodward – is to be burnt alive inside a huge wicker man. That's the order, anyhow, of mad-eyed pagan high-priest Christopher Lee. Howie has come to an isolated Hebridean island to investigate the disappearance of a young girl. The whole thing is a ruse. By some miracle of pagan thinking, as a representative of the queen he is to be sacrificed to the old gods. His death is to be in the manner first described by that great propagandist Julius Caesar, writing about the Celts, in his *Commentary on the Gallic Wars*.

The wooden frame of the Wicker Man is set ablaze and the head rolls off in a famous shot where the flaming ball of the sun sinking in the sky seems to replace it. The shot was a pure and incandescent fluke, and far from being the May Day event that everyone supposes, the entire cast was sucking ice-cubes so their breath couldn't be seen in the late October chill.

There are more legends swirling around *The Wicker Man* than perhaps any other film. The matter is not helped when the actors and crew seem to remember the same events in a totally different way. In the close-ups of Woodward struggling inside the Wicker Man itself, Woodward recalls that he was reading from crib-sheets painted in huge letters on the nearby cliffs. The director Robin Hardy, on the other hand, has no recollection of this at all, and he also denies Woodward's assertion that producers arrived from America to close the production down in the last few days.

There were in fact two Wicker Men built for the final scene; the large one in which Woodward is imprisoned, and a much smaller one, built about 500 yards away, that is set alight. In the original drawings both structures had eyes made white with bunched daisies. Both were made from lumber shipped up from London, and the second was drenched in flammable creosote. The legs of this one, encased in concrete to stop it falling over prematurely, are still a tourist attraction on the cliffs of Burrowhead in south-western Scotland (ironically near to St Ninian's cave – where Christianity was first brought to Scotland).

Despite the myths, Woodward was never in any real danger during the scene. A crane or cherrypicker was behind him all the time, just

out of shot, and he was also attached to a piece of stuntman safety kit called a Kirby Wire. Indeed, once he was filmed entering the larger Wicker Man, he climbed out again and a stuntman took over. The close-ups were all filmed on the final day in the second, smaller edifice. Up until the very last minute on 26th October 1972 it was not clear whether the final shot was possible.

Art director Seamus Flannery recalls that one of the camera operators 'just grabbed his camera and sprinted' when the clouds suddenly and unexpectedly parted and the sun blazed forth.

WITHNAIL & I
1987
DIRECTED BY BRUCE ROBINSON

> *"DON'T ATTEMPT ANYTHING WITHOUT THE GLOVES!"*

Richard E Grant is having a crisis come-down after a 60-hour drinking binge – and it isn't a pretty sight. Then again, neither is the Camden flat where he lives with the 'I' of the title, played by Paul McGann, who is about to rummage through the most disgusting sink-full of unwashed plates imaginable.

It's a flat that has gone down in pop-culture legend as the fragrant, baroque pinnacle of derelict and decaying student digs: dirty, dank, piled with empty wine bottles and teeming with vermin. A soiled dingy curtain hangs in the kitchen. A soiled dingy pair of Y-fronts hangs off Richard E Grant. 'The entire sink's gone rotten,' cries Grant in alarm.

The thing is, they really didn't have to act. For a number of production reasons the flat had been left to fester and it was all Richard E Grant and Paul McGann could do to keep their breakfast down.

The director Bruce Robinson had based his script on his youthful friendship with a fellow cash-strapped actor called Vivian MacKerrell. He had a clear idea of the flat he wanted to create because he had lived in one just like it in 1969, the year in which *Withnail & I* is set.

Production designer Michael Pickwoad actually used a large Bayswater house for the location shot, just before it was about to be renovated. In the derelict kitchen he lined the windowsill with old milk bottles filled with varying degrees of soured milk. On the Sunday before filming began, Pickwoad's team was dispatched to buy dozens of Chinese takeaways, which were smeared over a number of chipped plates and left to dry on the balcony.

These were then stacked in the sink with a certain amount of liberated sweet-and-sour pork, teabags and fried rice. Due to a number of production delays, the scene – scheduled to be filmed on Monday – didn't actually happen till mid-morning on Wednesday. With the heat of the lights cranked up, the camera crew were beginning to

retch and threatened a walk-out as the kitchen sink started to bubble with a horrifyingly rank grey gloop.

Paul McGann has to put on the gloves to do the washing up. The script had called for a 'naso-visual' horror – and that was exactly what they got.

'I think we've been in here too long,' says Withnail, gagging. 'I feel unusual.' The scene was hastily wrapped as cast and crew ran head-long into the fresh air.

The caterers were not much needed that day.

THE WIZARD OF OZ
1939
DIRECTED BY VICTOR FLEMING

How did a deleted scene from *The Wizard of Oz* come to hold all the clues to David Lynch's *Mulholland Drive*?

The Wizard of Oz, the 1939 film starring Judy Garland, originally featured an elaborate dance number called 'The Jitterbug'. Costing $80,000 to make and taking five weeks to shoot, it was part of a larger subplot which was jettisoned in earlier script rewrites, and included characters called Princess Betty and the Grand Duke of Oz.

In the lost Jitterbug scene, Dorothy, the Scarecrow, the Cowardly Lion and the Tin Man are on their way to the Witch's castle, when they are attacked by the evil bugs in the Haunted Woods. They are described by those who saw the original footage as seemingly pink and blue mosquito-like 'rascals' that give one 'the jitters' (either by actually biting people or simply by their annoying, invasive buzz).

All that remains of this deleted dance number is an amateur recording of it being filmed, with the set technicians visibly manipulating the 'haunted' trees which boast great twig-like hands and all four actors singing and dancing. It's the most jazz-influenced of all the original songs, written by Harold Arlen who also shot this extant amateur footage.

When, after its first LA preview, the movie was judged to be 20 minutes too long by producer Mervyn LeRoy, the Jitterbug scene was the first to go. It's said the producers were worried that a fashionable dance craze might date the film.

What's far more likely is that they discovered the Jitterbug's inalienable cultural association with alcohol misuse and mixed-race Harlem dives (witness Cab Calloway's hedonistic short film *Jitterbug Party* from 1935). From the extant footage, the *Oz* Jitterbug scene has a wild and abandoned quality quite at odds with the rest of the film. The Jitterbug was all about getting drunk.

The scene was part of the finished print in that first San Bernardino screening, but when it was removed from the film, the footage appears to have been lost. References to the deleted scene remain, with the Wicked Witch ordering to 'send the insects ahead to soften them up' and the Lion at one point sporting a huge bug sprayer.

And the Lynch connection? David Lynch has filled his movies with

references to *The Wizard of Oz* (especially *Wild at Heart*), but *Mulholland Drive* actually opens with a stylised, fanciful Jitterbug dance sequence. It's the beginning of a whole dream/attack/transportation motif which has kept people guessing about the hidden meanings of Lynch's movie ever since.

Dorothy's lost words still apply to many an *ingénue* in Hollywood, and the lure of drink, drugs and dreams: 'So be careful/of that rascal/keep away from/the Jitterbug'. Judy Garland never did beat the Jitterbug, dying of an accidental drug overdose at the age of 47.

WOMEN IN LOVE
1969
DIRECTED BY KEN RUSSELL

A fire crackles in the grate of a castle room. Alan Bates is wearing a shaggy beard – and no clothes. Oliver Reed is wearing a louche handlebar moustache – and no clothes. They're wrestling naked in the famous scene in Ken Russell's *Women in Love*. And it's a scene that nearly didn't happen, thanks to Russell's own doubts about getting it past the censor and both actors producing sick notes from their doctors at the eleventh hour.

Adapted from the novel by DH Lawrence and set in 1920s England, Glenda Jackson won a best actress Oscar for her portrayal of the free-thinking artist at the centre of the film. Alan Bates plays the DH Lawrence character, a schools inspector who seeks 'pure' relation-ships with men and women.

His best friend happens to be the wealthy local coal-mine owner Gerald, played with beetling intensity by Oliver Reed. It's in Gerald's stately home – the semi-derelict Elvaston Castle in Derby – where the two men strip off for a good roll around (all in the name of chaste male bonding, you understand). The roaring fire made the set incredibly hot, according to cinematographer Billy Williams, who used two hand-held cameras to film it bathed in an orange, filtered light.

According to Ken Russell, the scene was not in the original script. On mentioning his worries about tackling the UK censors to a customarily inebriated Oliver Reed in his own kitchen, Reed wrestled the director to the floor and made him swear to include it.

However, despite this gung-ho early enthusiasm, Reed's interest in actually doing the scene dwindled as the fateful hour approached. Bates too seemed worried. The day before the shoot Reed had developed a limp and Bates sniffled with a cold, both producing medical certificates to prove they were unable to perform.

Russell prepared an alternative set and scene should both men refuse to film the scene, but in the end the two of them strode into the baronial hall at 8.30 that morning and disrobed – 'proud as peacocks', according to the director. What had changed? During their pub binge the night before, frequent visits to the urinals had enabled both actors to, ahem, compare notes.

Relieved to establish that neither was substantially better endowed than the other, the actors slapped each other on the back and decided to do the scene.

YOU ONLY LIVE TWICE
1967
DIRECTED BY LEWIS GILBERT

One of the highlights of the fifth film in the James Bond series was the 'Little Nellie' autogyro aircraft. After Q comes over from England to deliver it, Sean Connery takes the opportunity to pilot Little Nellie to a remote area of Japan on a reconnaissance mission. However, the extraordinary aerial shots by legendary cameraman John Jordan came at a heavy price, and what happened above the mountains of Miyazaki was to contribute to his early death.

The autogyro used in this film was piloted by its inventor Ken Wallis – a former Wing Commander in the RAF and an experienced pilot (during the 1950s he regularly flew B-36 bombers with a nuclear payload) and, in his mid-90s, the holder of more than 30 world records. Production designer Ken Adam had heard him talking on the radio and promptly hired him.

John Stear's special effects team then adorned the autogyro with missiles and machine guns. This did nothing to help the stability of the frantic little machine, and it was clear from the beginning that it was going to be hard to handle. Above the skies of Japan, Wallis nearly crashed into the camera on several occasions. There were five hours of filmed flight and 85 take-offs recorded.

John Jordan had developed his own technique of hanging dangerously from a harness, buffeted by wind, feet resting on the helicopter landing strut. But during the sequence when Little Nellie is attacked by two Bell 47 helicopters one of the Bell blades hit his foot, almost cutting it off. As luck would have it there was a microsurgery conference in town, and the best surgeons in the world were able to re-attach the foot. But when he got back to London Jordan had it amputated, feeling that it was 'not quite right'.

Now sporting a prosthetic foot, Jordan continue undaunted for the three years following by filming some of the best landscape shots in *On her Majesty's Secret Service*, and actually taking his foot off to film the high-speed bobsleigh shots. A year after filming that Bond film, he was dead. While lensing action footage from a B25 Mitchell Bomber in 1969 over the Pacific he fell two thousand feet to his death, his ability to keep a sure footing impaired by his prosthetic limb. *Catch 22* was the last thing he ever worked on.

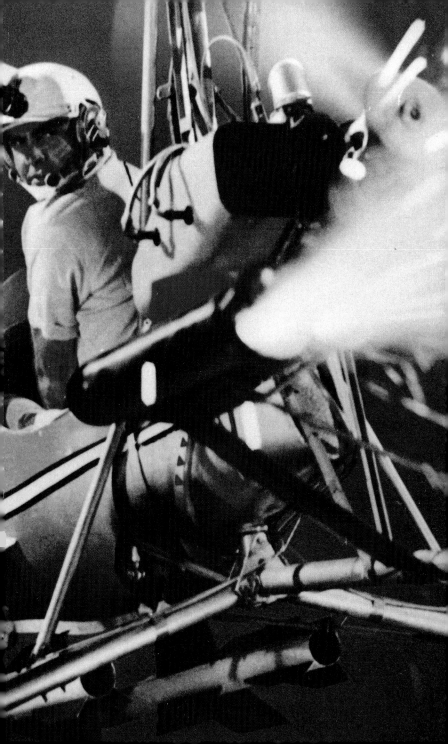

CREDITS

ALIEN: 20TH CENTURY FOX / THE KOBAL COLLECTION
AMADEUS: SAUL ZAENTZ COMPANY / THE KOBAL COLLECTION
APOCALYPSE NOW: ZOETROPE/UNITED ARTISTS / THE KOBAL COLLECTION
BASIC INSTINCT: CAROLCO / THE KOBAL COLLECTION
BATTLESHIP POTEMKIN, THE: GOSKINO / THE KOBAL COLLECTION
BIRDS, THE: UNIVERSAL / THE KOBAL COLLECTION
BLADE RUNNER: LADD COMPANY/WARNER BROS / THE KOBAL COLLECTION
BLUE VELVET: DE LAURENTIIS / THE KOBAL COLLECTION
BONFIRE OF THE VANITIES: WARNER HOME VIDEO
BREATHLESS: EVERETT COLLECTION INC
BULLITT: WARNER BROS / THE KOBAL COLLECTION
BUTCH CASSIDY AND THE SUNDANCE KID: 20TH CENTURY FOX / THE KOBAL
    COLLECTION
CAPE FEAR: UNIVERSAL / THE KOBAL COLLECTION
CARRIE: UNITED ARTISTS / THE KOBAL COLLECTION
CHIEN ANDALOU, UN: BUNUEL-DALI / THE KOBAL COLLECTION
CASABLANCA: WARNER BROS / THE KOBAL COLLECTION / WOODS, JACK
CHARGE OF THE LIGHT BRIGADE, THE: WARNER BROS / THE KOBAL
    COLLECTION
CHARIOTS OF FIRE: 20TH CENTURY FOX/ALLIED STARS/ENIGMA / THE KOBAL
    COLLECTION
CHINATOWN: PARAMOUNT / THE KOBAL COLLECTION
CLOCKWORK ORANGE, A: WARNER BROS / THE KOBAL COLLECTION
CONQUEROR, THE: RKO / THE KOBAL COLLECTION
CROW, THE: PRESSMAN/MOST / THE KOBAL COLLECTION
DAY THE EARTH STOOD STILL, THE: 20TH CENTURY FOX / THE KOBAL
    COLLECTION
DELIVERANCE: WARNER BROS / THE KOBAL COLLECTION / HAMILTON, JOHN
DON'T LOOK NOW: CASEY PRODS-ELDORADO FILMS / THE KOBAL COLLECTION
DR. NO: DANJAQ/EON/UA / THE KOBAL COLLECTION
EASY RIDER: COLUMBIA / THE KOBAL COLLECTION
ELEPHANT MAN, THE: PARAMOUNT / THE KOBAL COLLECTION
ENIGMA OF KASPAR HAUSER, THE: FILMVERLAG DER AUTOREN / THE KOBAL
    COLLECTION
EXORCIST, THE: WARNER BROS / THE KOBAL COLLECTION
FOUR FEATHERS: UNITED ARTISTS / THE KOBAL COLLECTION
GLADIATOR: DREAMWORKS/UNIVERSAL / THE KOBAL COLLECTION /
    BUITENDIJK, JAAP
GODFATHER, THE: SUNSET BOULEVARD / CORBIS
GRADUATE, THE: EMBASSY/LAURENCE TURMAN / THE KOBAL COLLECTION
GREAT ESCAPE, THE: MIRISCH/UNITED ARTISTS / THE KOBAL COLLECTION
HEAVEN'S GATE: UNITED ARTISTS / THE KOBAL COLLECTION
HIGH NOON: STANLEY KRAMER/UNITED ARTISTS / THE KOBAL COLLECTION
IN THE HEAT OF THE NIGHT: MIRISCH/UNITED ARTISTS / THE KOBAL
    COLLECTION
ITALIAN JOB, THE: PARAMOUNT / THE KOBAL COLLECTION
JAWS: UNIVERSAL / THE KOBAL COLLECTION
LAWRENCE OF ARABIA: COLUMBIA / THE KOBAL COLLECTION

LIFE OF BRIAN: ALAMY IMAGES
LORD OF THE RINGS, THE: THE TWO TOWERS: NEW LINE CINEMA / THE KOBAL
COLLECTION
MATRIX RELOADED, THE: WARNER BROS / THE KOBAL COLLECTION
METROPOLIS: UFA / THE KOBAL COLLECTION
MISSION, THE: WARNER BROS / THE KOBAL COLLECTION
OLD BOY: FINECUT
ONCE UPON A TIME IN THE WEST: PARAMOUNT/RAFRAN / THE KOBAL
COLLECTION
ON THE WATERFRONT: COLUMBIA / THE KOBAL COLLECTION
PERFORMANCE: WARNER/GOODTIMES / THE KOBAL COLLECTION
POLTERGEIST: MGM/SLA ENTERTAINMENT / THE KOBAL COLLECTION
PRETTY WOMAN: TOUCHSTONE/WARNERS / THE KOBAL COLLECTION
PSYCHO: PARAMOUNT / THE KOBAL COLLECTION / CREAMER, WILLIAM
RAIDERS OF THE LOST ARK: LUCASFILM LTD/PARAMOUNT / THE KOBAL
COLLECTION
RAISE THE TITANIC: INCORPORATED TELEVISION COMPANY
RESERVOIR DOGS: LIVE ENTERTAINMENT / THE KOBAL COLLECTION
ROSEMARY'S BABY: PARAMOUNT / THE KOBAL COLLECTION
SCARFACE: UNIVERSAL / THE KOBAL COLLECTION SEVENTH SEAL: SVENSK
FILMINDUSTRI
SEVEN YEAR ITCH, THE: 20TH CENTURY FOX / THE KOBAL COLLECTION / SHAW,
SAM
SHINING, THE: WARNER BROS / THE KOBAL COLLECTION
SINGIN' IN THE RAIN: MGM / THE KOBAL COLLECTION
SOLDIER BLUE: AVCO EMBASSY / THE KOBAL COLLECTION
SOME LIKE IT HOT: UNITED ARTISTS / THE KOBAL COLLECTION
SOUND OF MUSIC, THE: 20TH CENTURY FOX / THE KOBAL COLLECTION
SPARTACUS: BRYNA/UNIVERSAL / THE KOBAL COLLECTION
SPARTACUS: BRYNA/UNIVERSAL / THE KOBAL COLLECTION
STAIRCASE: 20TH CENTURY FOX / THE KOBAL COLLECTION
STAR WARS EPISODE IV: A NEW HOPE: LUCASFILM/20TH CENTURY FOX / THE
KOBAL COLLECTION
TAXI DRIVER: COLUMBIA / THE KOBAL COLLECTION
TERMINATOR, THE: ORION / THE KOBAL COLLECTION
TWIGHLIGHT ZONE: BETTMANN / CORBIS
UN CHIEN ANDALOU: BUNUEL-DALI / THE KOBAL COLLECTION
VAMPIRE'S KISS: MGM ENTERTAINMENT
WHATEVER HAPPENED TO BABY JANE: BETTMAN / CORBIS
WHEN HARRY MET SALLY: CASTLE ROCK/NELSON/COLUMBIA / THE KOBAL
COLLECTION
WICKER MAN, THE: BRITISH LION / THE KOBAL COLLECTION
WITHNAIL AND I: HANDMADE FILMS / THE KOBAL COLLECTION
WIZARD OF OZ, THE: MGM / THE KOBAL COLLECTION
WOMEN IN LOVE: UNITED ARTISTS / THE KOBAL COLLECTION
YOU ONLY LIVE TWICE: DANJAQ/EON/UA / THE KOBAL COLLECTION

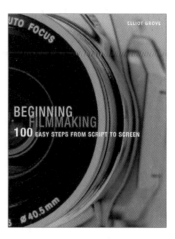

3ºº   Gen 2/16 70